# Open Mind

## Upper Intermediate Workbook

Mike Boyle
Anna Osborn

Concept Development:
Mariela Gil Vierma

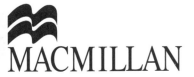

MACMILLAN

Macmillan Education
4 Crinan Street
London N1 9XW
A division of Macmillan Publishers Limited

Companies and representatives throughout the world

ISBN 978-0-230-45834-5 with key
ISBN 978-0-230-45852-9 without key

This edition published 2015
First edition published 2010

Designed by emc design limited
Illustrated by Sally Elford p55
Cover designed by emc design limited
Cover photograph courtesy of Getty Images/Paul Bradbury (Foreground), Getty Images/lpbb (Background).
Picture research by Victoria Gaunt

The authors would like to thank the schools, teachers and students whose input has been invaluable in preparing this new edition. They would also like to thank the editorial and design teams at Macmillan for doing such a great job of organising the material and bringing it to life.

The publishers would like to thank the following educators and institutions who reviewed materials and provided us with invaluable insight and feedback for the development of Open Mind:

Petra Florianová, Gymnázium, Praha 6, Arabská 14; Inés Frigerio, Universidad Nacional de Río Cuarto; Alison Greenwood, University of Bologna, Centro Linguistico di Ateneo; Roumyana Yaneva Ivanova, The American College of Sofia; Tá a Jan a íková, SOŠ Drtinova Prague; Mari Carmen Lafuente, Escuela Oficial de Idiomas Hospitalet, Barcelona; Alice Lockyer, Pompeu Fabra University; Javier Roque Sandro Majul, Windmill School of English; Paul Neale, Susan Carol Owens and Beverley Anne Sharp, Cambridge Academy of English; Audrey Renton, Dubai Men's College, Higher Colleges of Technology, UAE; Martin Stanley, British Council, Bilbao; Luiza Wójtowicz-Waga, Warsaw Study Centre; Escuela Oficial de Idiomas de Getxo; Cámara de Comercio de Bilbao; Universidad Autónoma de Bellaterra; Escuela Oficial de Idiomas EOI de Barcelona; University of Barcelona; Escuela Oficial de Idiomas Sant Gervasi; Isidro Almedarez, Deniz Atesok, Monica Delgadillo, Elaine Hodgson, Mark Lloyd, Rufus Vaughan-Spruce, Kristof van Houdt, Rob Duncan, James Conboy, Jonathan Danby, Fiona Craig, Martin Guilfoyle, Rodrigo Rosa.

The authors and publishers would like to thank the following for permission to reproduce the following material.

Extract from 'Jamie Oliver wants childhood obesity at the top of the political agenda' by Richard Garner. Originally published in The Independent on 25.04.2014 © The Independent, 2014. Reprinted with permission. www.theindependent.co.uk, Extract from 'Winston Churchill didn't really exist say teens' by Aislinn Simpson © Telegraph Group Limited 2008, first published in the Daily Telegraph 4 February 2008. Reprinted by permission of the publisher. www.telegraph.co.uk, Material adapted from 'Water Footprints' published on the Water Footprint Network, www.waterfootprint.org, Extract from 'What's frying at Walkie Scorchie?' by Harry Wallop © Telegraph Group Limited 2013, first published in the Daily Telegraph 3 September 2013. Reprinted by permission of the publisher. www.telegraph.co.uk, Material adapted from 'The Science of Competition' by Kara Miller & Kinnie Chapin, first published by WGBH News as a part of the WGBH Innovation hub http://blogs.wgbh.org/innovation-hub/, Extract from 'Does it matter if children don't care about winning?' by Les Roopanarine. Originally published in The Guardian on 26 April 2014 © Guardian News and Media Limited, 2014. Reprinted with permission. www.theguardian.com/uk, Material adapted from 'Selfie City'. Reprinted with permission. http://selfiecity.net/, Extract from 'The death of photography: are camera phones destroying an artform?' by Stuart Jeffries © Guardian News & Media Ltd 2013. First published in the Guardian 13 December 2013. Reprinted with permission. www.theguardian.com, Extract adapted from 'The Five Lost Cities of the Future'. First published on Scribol. Used with permission. www.scribol.com

The authors and publishers would like to thank the following for permission to reproduce their photographs:

Alamy/Angela Hampton Picture Library p57, Alamy/billdayone p35(tr), Alamy/Blend Images p69, Alamy/Cultura Creative p6(t), Alamy/David Bleeker Photography p30(br), Alamy/Phil Degginger p74(tl), Alamy/Lev Dolgachov p11, Alamy/epa european pressphoto agency b.v. p38(d), Alamy/Hero Images Inc. p22, Alamy/Huntstock, Inc p54, Alamy/Image Source Plus p48, Alamy/Sebastian Kaulitzki p53, Alamy/Fredrick Kippe p19, Alamy/Dan Leeth p29(br), Alamy/Christian Musat p74(tl), Alamy/National Geographic Image Collection p62(cr), Alamy/Susan & Allan Parker p58, Alamy/Purcell Team p29(tr), Alamy/Radius Images p33, Alamy/Simon Reddy p70, Alamy/Jack Sullivan p31(br), Alamy/John Warburton-Lee p15, Alamy/Westend61 GmbH p18, Alamy/Matthew Williams-Ellis p24; Bananastock p26(cr); Corbis p34, Corbis/Atlantide Phototravel p44, Corbis/KidStock/Blend Images p50(b), Corbis/Blend Images/Paul Burns p61, Corbis/Reuters/ALEX GRIMM p52, Corbis/Transtock/John Lamm p43(t), Corbis/National Geographic Society/Andy Olson p51, Corbis/Dallas Morning News/Smiley N. Pool p73, Corbis/Blend Images/John Lund/Marc Romanelli p27, Corbis/Ocean/Chris Ryan p36(cl), Corbis/Blend Images/Vladimir Serov p65(tr), Corbis/Blend Images/Inti St Clair p10(3), Corbis/beyond/Yevgen Timashov p65(tl), Corbis/Demotix/umar87 p60, Corbis/Somos Images/Bill Varie p16, Corbis/Wavebreak Media Ltd p46; Getty Images/Carlo A p4, Getty Images/AFP p74, Getty Images/andresr p66, Getty Images/Bloomberg p17, Getty Images/Brand New Images p5(c), Getty Images/Tristan Brown p72, Getty Images/Design Pics/Colleen Cahill p10(4), Getty Images/Jeffrey Coolidge p40, Getty Images/Nick David p65(br), Getty Images/Eric Raptosh Photography p7(tl), Getty Images/EyeWire p56, Getty Images/Cesare Ferrari p68, Getty Images/ilbusca p59, Getty Images/Andrew Ilyasov p62(b), Getty Images/Daniel Ingold p65(cr), Getty Images/Christian Kober p38(a), Getty Images/Lambert p20, Getty Images/Design Pics/Diane Levit p28(tr), Getty Images/Bertrand Linet p38(c), Getty Images/Iain Masterton p29(cr), Getty Images/mediaphotos p25, Getty Images/Zoran Milich p67(b), Getty Images/Erin Patrice O'Brien p6(b), Getty Images/Jose Luis Pelaez Inc p35(br), Getty Images/Eric Gregory Powell p28(cr), Getty Images/Radius Images p26(tcr), Getty Images/Vikram Raghuvanshi p7(br), Getty Images/David Ramos p38(e), Getty Images/Gregor Schuster p12, Getty Images/Inti St Clair p14, Getty Images/AFP/ Stringer p38(b), Getty Images/Travelpix Ltd p74 , Getty Images/Tuan Tran p67(a), Getty Images/Westend61 p10(2), Getty Images/Barry Willis p43(br), Getty Images/WPA Pool p42, Getty Images/XiXinXing p64(tl), Getty Images/Stephen Zeigler p26(tr); Glow Images p10(1); ImageSource pp10(4), 16; Photodisc p74; Plainpicture/Cultura p30(t); Press Association Images/KAREL PRINSLO p50(t), Press Association Image/Andy Scofield/PA Archives pp45(background), 45(insert); Superstock/Image Source p8; Thinkstock/iStock/AmmentorpDK p31(tr), Thinkstock/biglike p64(tr), Thinkstock/ROBERTO CAUCINO p63, Thinkstock/Feverpitched p36(tr), Thinkstock/izustun p64(b), Thinkstock/monkeybusinessimages p23, Thinkstock/Paul p26(b), Thinkstock/Rauluminate p5(b), Thinkstock/scanrail p5(tr), Thinkstock/TongRo Images p32, Thinkstock/Vilches p75, Corbis/Wavebreak Media Ltd p49.

Printed and bound in Spain by Edelvives

2018  2017  2016  2015
10 9 8 7 6 5 4 3 2 1

# CONTENTS

# UNIT 1 WHO DO YOU THINK YOU ARE?

## 1 READING: for different purposes

### 1 FUTURE IDENTITIES: Changing identities in the next ten years
#### EXECUTIVE SUMMARY

Identity is changing. Over the next ten years, people's identities are likely to be significantly affected by hyper-connectivity (where people can be constantly connected online), the spread of social media and the increase in online personal information.

What does identity mean today?

- PEOPLE HAVE MANY OVERLAPPING IDENTITIES
  This report considers several aspects of identities including country, religion, family background and social status. A person can have all of these identities at the same time. For example, at home a person may find their identity as a parent most important, while at work they might identify most as an employee. Online their sense of identity may be connected to a hobby.

- PEOPLE EXPRESS THEIR IDENTITIES IN DIFFERENT WAYS
  On the internet, it is easier for people to adopt an identity that is different from the way in which others stereotype them. Some people even feel that they have achieved their 'true' identity for the first time online. For example, some people may socialise more successfully, and express themselves more freely, online. This is one of the ways in which online identities can transform offline identities.

- IDENTITIES HAVE VALUE
  People's identities have personal, social and commercial value. As more personal data is stored online, there is the potential for positive social interaction, but also for criminal exploitation or misuse.

Information source: http://www.bis.gov.uk

### 2 Expressing (and protecting!) your online identity – By Mark Mayes

**MARK:** Is it a good idea for young people to be on social media?

**LIZ:** Yes and no. You can find people who have similar interests, and you can express who you really are, with pictures, blogs and more.

**MARK:** Those are the good things. What is the downside?

**LIZ:** Well, we all change over time, but this is particularly true for young people; you're not the same person at 20 as you were at 15. That can be a problem because things you put online now may be embarrassing in a few years.

**MARK:** Are there other dangers?

**LIZ:** Yes. Young people need to remember that we have multiple identities. You may see yourself as a future pop star, for example, but you're also a student, an employee and a brother or sister or family member. It's very easy for the wrong person to see something. For example, if you complain about your teachers online, the college you want to go to might see that and it doesn't look good.

**MARK:** What about bullying?

**LIZ:** It's a real risk for young people. It's harder to control your identity online because anyone can post information about you. People can say hurtful and untrue things about you. But overall, I think social media is a great thing for young people if it's used carefully.

It's a real risk for young people.

4

## A Look quickly at the two texts. Then answer the questions.

1 Where is each text from? Write the letter of the source next to each text number.

Text 1 ___  Text 2 ___

a) a magazine article
b) a textbook
c) a novel
d) a government report

2 Why would we read each text? Write the letter of the reason next to each text number. There may be more than one reason for each text.

Text 1 ___  Text 2 ___

a) for pleasure
b) for information
c) to find out opinions
d) to find out news

## B Read the texts in Exercise A again. Choose T (true) or F (false) for each statement.

1 Technology hasn't changed identity in the last ten years.          T / F
2 Most people have the same identity in all situations.              T / F
3 Some people find it easier to express their true identity online.  T / F
4 Your identity can be worth money to some people.                   T / F
5 Only you can change and control your online identity.              T / F
6 People need to think about who might see their information online.  T / F

# 2 VOCABULARY: personal identity

## A Choose the correct options to complete the article.

### We ask, you answer!

**Today's question:**
What influences your identity?

**MATT, 41** | ● click to listen
Wow, that's a tough question! I think when I was younger, my friends really shaped who I was, so the **(1)** social status / social group I was part of was very important. Also I had a lot of big **(2)** life goals / family values back then. I wanted to be a musician, so music was my life and really influenced my identity. But things are different now. I'm a husband and a dad – that's how I see myself. So I guess **(3)** family values / family background are more important to my sense of identity now.

**YASMIN, 20** | ● click to listen
Well, I've thought a lot about this since I came to study in the UK. In the Middle East, where I come from, a lot of people get a **(4)** value / sense of identity from their **(5)** family background / life goals. Not just your parents, but your grandparents and even great-grandparents show people who you are. If you come from a 'good' family, your **(6)** social group / social status is higher and people treat you better. Now, I still think family is a really important factor in your identity but it's not the only thing. The subject you study, your friends and interests are factors, too.

## B 🎧 01 Listen and check your answers.

## 3 COMMUNICATION STRATEGY: agreeing and disagreeing

**A**  **02 Listen to a debate on a radio programme. Tick the person that makes each point.**

|   |   | Mark Owens | Lisa Adams |
|---|---|---|---|
| 1 | It is good to buy cool clothes for children. | ☐ | ☐ |
| 2 | Children need to be part of a social group. | ☐ | ☐ |
| 3 | Children need comfortable clothes, not designer clothes. | ☐ | ☐ |
| 4 | Children should be allowed to look good if they want to. | ☐ | ☐ |
| 5 | Many parents can't afford to buy designer clothes for their children. | ☐ | ☐ |
| 6 | Personality, not clothes, helps develop a child's sense of identity. | ☐ | ☐ |

**B Listen again. Put the phrases for agreeing and disagreeing in the order that you hear them (1–6).**

☐ I couldn't agree more.
☐ Yes and no.
☐ In a sense, you're right.
☐ Well, yes, to a certain extent, but …
☐ I'm sorry, but I just don't think that's true.
☐ I'm afraid I can't agree.

## 4 GRAMMAR: review of past tenses

**A Tick the sentences that refer to actions or states in progress in the past.**

1 ☐ Kim was studying in Europe during the winter holidays.
2 ☐ Fareed had read the book before he saw the film.
3 ☐ Don't worry, Marisol. We weren't talking about you.
4 ☐ Mia did prepare for the interview, but it wasn't enough.

**B Choose the correct options to complete the comments.**

### WHAT'S RIGHT?

Ⓧ I was having to wear a uniform when I was at school.

✓ _____
_____

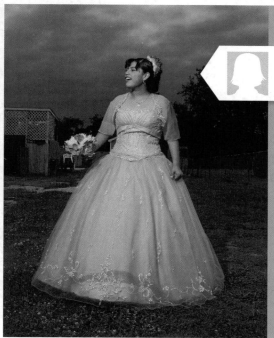

**LUISA POSTED A PHOTO**

This was me at my big quinceañera (15th birthday party). Look at what I **(1)** was wearing / had worn! They say the quinceañera is when you become an adult. Ha ha!

**JACOB:**
I think you look nice! I **(2)** wasn't having / didn't have a big party for my 15th, but I **(3)** did had / did have a big one for my 16th. I **(4)** didn't look like / wasn't looking like an adult, either.

**NATALIA:**
Ha ha, you should see my quinceañera pictures. I **(5)** was never wearing / had never worn makeup before that day, so I **(6)** put on / did put on way too much. I really **(7)** did feel / had felt grown-up, though!

## 5 VOCABULARY: *sense*

**A** Look at the words and phrases in bold in the sentences. Write N (noun), V (verb) or A (adjective).

1 ____ Maria said the book changed her life, but I found it confusing and couldn't **make sense of** it.
2 ____ My friends always **sense** when I'm feeling low.
3 ____ No one was surprised that Tom wore shorts when it was so cold. He doesn't have any **common sense**.
4 ____ I've always been a **sensitive** person and try to understand how other people are feeling.
5 ____ Instead of being **sensible** and studying business, Louise took classes in art and philosophy.
6 ____ Don't ask Diego about his family. They don't get along, so it's a **sensitive** topic.
7 ____ Sophia's best quality is her **sense of humour**. She can always make people laugh.

**B** Complete this magazine excerpt with the correct form of the words and phrases in bold from Exercise A.

### My many identities

posted by Daniel
3 days ago

I've been reading a government report on the future of identity. It's fascinating, although some parts are a bit technical and it's difficult to **(1)** _____ them. According to the report, no one has just one identity. We all have different identities in different situations. Here are a few of mine!

- At university: I'm Daniel the class clown. People say I have a great **(2)** _____ and everyone loves my jokes – well, except for the teachers!
- At work: I'm an intern at a big company and I want a job there after I've graduated. People there see my **(3)** _____ side – I always find reasonable, practical solutions to problems. My boss says I'm the only one there who has any **(4)** _____.
- With my friends, I'm known as a **(5)** _____ person who listens well and gives good advice. I can **(6)** _____ when my friends are upset and I'm always there for them. My friends can talk to me about anything. No topic is too **(7)** _____!

## 6 GRAMMAR: *would, be + always, used to*

### WHAT'S RIGHT?

(✗) I always was taking pictures to express myself.

(✓) _____

**A** Look at the structures. Write *PP* if the structure is used to talk about the present or past and *P* if it's used to talk about the past only.

1 ____ *would (always/never)* + base form
2 ____ *(always/never) used to* + base form
3 ____ *be always + –ing* form

**B** Rewrite Nicole's comments using the structure in brackets.

'When I was young, **(1)** I tried to be part of the "cool" group. **(2)** I did what my friends told me to do, and **(3)** I often behaved irresponsibly. **(4)** I didn't have a strong sense of my own identity and, as a result, **(5)** I didn't feel confident.'

1 (*used to*) *I used to try to be part of the 'cool' group.*
2 (*would/always*) _____
3 (*be/always*) _____
4 (*never/used to*) _____
5 (*would/never*) _____

**C** Complete the story with the correct form of the phrases from the box. You can use some phrases more than once and, in some cases, more than one answer is possible.

| always do | always make sure | never help | never take | work |
|---|---|---|---|---|

'It's funny how things change. I remember how, when I was really young, my father **(1)** _____ away from home a lot. Because of this, he **(2)** _____ my mum in the house or play with us. In contrast, my mum was the typical responsible wife and mother. She **(3)** _____ housework and she **(4)** _____ we had what we needed. She **(5)** _____ time off or relax. But nowadays, Dad works nearby, so he stays home while she goes out and has fun. It's great!'

# SkillsStudio

**A  Read the text quickly. Then choose the correct options to complete the statements.**

1  According to the text, there is one / there are many possible definitions of the word 'identity.'
2  The text says that a person can have only one / more than one identity, depending on the situation.
3  Everyone has three / one of three main types of identity, according to the text.

**B  Read the text again and choose the correct sentence for each gap. There is one extra sentence that you do not need to use.**

A  These include identities such as family relationships, friendships, membership of communities and attachment to particular places.
B  There are several reasons why identities are important for policy makers in government.
C  They can also be *exclusive*, defined by *not* being a member of a particular group.
D  However, others have the potential to change over time, or may remain the same (such as national identity or attachment to places where people live or work).
E  These can be used to verify that people are who they say they are.
F  There is, therefore, no single definition of 'identity' that everyone agrees upon.

**C  Read the text again and answer these questions.**

1  In the second paragraph, what is the main point about identities?
   a)  Your identity is created and controlled mostly by other people.
   b)  Every identity is unique and no two people have the same one.
   c)  The main way identities are formed is by rejection from a social group.
   d)  Identities have many parts and are formed in many different ways.
2  The word *rejection* in line 31 means …
   a)  a feeling of sadness.
   b)  including.
   c)  refusal to accept.
   d)  the choice to quit something.
3  Which of the following is an example of social identity?
   a)  being in a football team
   b)  having blond hair and blue eyes
   c)  earning a good salary
   d)  having a university degree
4  The word *distinct* in line 58 means …
   a)  obvious.
   b)  separate and different.
   c)  easily seen or heard.
   d)  excellent.
5  Having parents who are immigrants from another country is an example of …
   a)  social identity.
   b)  biographical identity.
   c)  biometric identity.
   d)  none of these.
6  In the last paragraph, what is the main point about identities?
   a)  The parts of a person's identity can change over time.
   b)  Friendship groups change more easily than gender or ethnicity.
   c)  A person's family roles are not the same thing as his or her identity.
   d)  Hobbies are an important part of many people's identities.

**D  You are applying for a study-abroad programme. As part of the application process, write an essay of about 200 words on the following topic: 'My personal identity: past, present, and future.'**

# 2.1 Definition of identity

1 A person's 'identity' can be defined as those characteristics that determine who a person is. This includes a person's perception of themself as similar to, or different from, other people, but identities can also be imposed by others.

5 Dictionary definitions of 'identity' are often based on a very simplistic notion of identity made popular during the 1950s by the developmental psychologist Erik Erikson. His concept suggested that identity is shaped by the interaction of three elements: a person's biological characteristics,

10 their psychology and their cultural context. Since then, however, identity has become a key concept in a wide range of academic subjects, including political science, the social sciences and the humanities, and definitions of identity have expanded as a result. **(1)** ——

15 These different interpretations have shown that identities are socially constructed and highly complex. Many different types of identity are now discussed, such as cultural identity, organisational identity and national identity. Even for an individual, there are many possible identities that overlap

20 and can change over time or in different circumstances. People, therefore, each have an identity that combines many different aspects about themselves and together these give them a sense of meaning in their lives.

Identities can be *elective* or chosen by a person, such as by

25 membership of a social group. They can also be *ascribed* or decided and controlled by others, for example, through data about a person collected by a supermarket. Identities can be *inclusive*, such as membership of a family, team, religion or other group. **(2)** —— Again, these identities can

30 be controlled by the individual or by others, for instance, through rejection from a group.

In general, there are three overlapping types of identities, social, biographical and biometric:

- SOCIAL IDENTITIES are generated through roles
35 and relationships between people and wider culture and society. **(3)** ——

- BIOGRAPHICAL IDENTITIES are identities that individuals might use to describe themselves to another or how they perceive themselves. These might include

40 national identity, as well as ethnicity and religion – although these also have a strong social role. Identities such as a professional role or financial status might also be considered biographical identities.

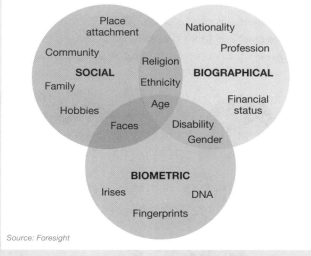

Fig 2.1: Types of identities: social, biographical and biometric identities, and some examples of each type.

*Source: Foresight*

- BIOMETRIC IDENTITIES are those aspects
45 of identity related to the body, including unique characteristics such as DNA, fingerprints, irises and faces. **(4)** ——

A person therefore has a sense of self that is constructed from many elements and these could be considered as

50 different 'identities'. Some aspects of an individual's identity are unlikely to change (gender, disability or ethnicity). Some types of identity change only very gradually over a person's lifetime (for example, age). **(5)** —— Other social identities can change more easily, for example, when

55 people belong to different communities (including online communities) or friendship groups. Some stages of life carry shifting family roles and responsibilities that create distinct identities, for example, being a child, being in a relationship, becoming a parent or grandparent, while

60 professional and financial identities can change as jobs, status, careers and experiences alter. People can also have identities related to hobbies, leisure and consumption, which for some people can change rapidly, while others maintain their 'hobbies' as an important part of themselves

65 over a long period of time.

# UNIT 2 GLOBAL VIEWS

## 1 LISTENING: understanding discourse markers

**A** 🎧 **03** Listen to four people describing their experiences of globalisation. Complete the sentences with the words from the box.

| communications   the economy   the service industry   trade |

1 Speaker 1 is discussing _____.
2 Speaker 2 is talking about _____.
3 Speaker 3 is concerned about _____.
4 Speaker 4 is describing _____.

**B** 🎧 **04** Listen again. Write the letters of the discourse markers (a–e) that each speaker uses.

Speaker 1 ___ ___ ___
Speaker 2 ___ ___ ___
Speaker 3 ___ ___ ___

**a)** like    **b)** kind of    **c)** well    **d)** you know    **e)** I mean

**C** 🎧 **05** Listen to Speaker 4 again. Complete the text with the discourse markers from Exercise B.

I think globalisation's great! I love using social networking sites because,
**(1)** _____, it **(2)** _____ means that I have friends all over the world now.
I have, **(3)** _____, 500 friends. It's really cool. **(4)** _____, they send me
photographs, music, videos – all kinds of stuff from their countries – and, **(5)** _____,
I send them things from my country, too. It's amazing.

## 2 VOCABULARY: globalisation

**A** Match the words or phrases (1–6) to their definitions (a–f).

1 economic growth (*n.*)       **a)** relating to a particular geographic area
2 profits (*n.*)                **b)** financial gains
3 multinational (*adj.*)        **c)** be in control of
4 regional (*adj.*)             **d)** an increase in the size of the economy
5 facilitate (*v.*)            **e)** make something easier
6 dominate (*v.*)              **f)** relating to more than two countries

**B** **Choose the correct options to complete the sentences.**

1   The company is multinational / regional with offices all over Europe,
    throughout the US and in Australia.
2   Globalisation has been good for the whole country because there's been
    economic growth / profits, which has led to a decrease in unemployment.
3   Large corporations facilitate / dominate the market, which means that small
    companies struggle to survive.
4   The company announced that they had made economic growth / profits of £3 million.
5   Right now, we only have a few multinational / regional offices in and around
    Birmingham but we're looking to expand into new areas next year.
6   Globalisation facilitates / dominates communication because it has become so much
    easier to talk to people on the other side of the world.

## 3 GRAMMAR: verbs with stative and dynamic uses

**A** **Complete the sentences with the correct form of the verb in brackets.**

1   I _____ (have) friends, family and colleagues around the world.
2   What time _____ (see) your parents?
3   I _____ (think) our city is losing its identity.
4   Multinational companies _____ (be) the largest employers in the city.

**B** **This comment contains five mistakes with stative and
dynamic verbs. Cross out the mistakes and write the correct form.**

 **LOVE ACROSS THE GLOBE**

My girlfriend and I had seen each other for three years when her
company offered her a job in the Shanghai office. It was being an amazing
opportunity, so she moved there last September, and we're not seeing
each other very often since then. It isn't being ideal but there are a lot of
ways to keep in touch. And we've just got engaged, so I'm thinking that
old saying, 'absence makes the heart grow fonder', might just be true!

**WHAT'S RIGHT?**

✗ I think of applying for a
transfer to the Stockholm
office next year.

✓ _____
_____
_____

## 4 GRAMMAR: repeated and double comparatives

**A  Match the two parts to make complete sentences.**

1  The more competition there is,
2  With new technology we can
3  More and more old people are
4  The more we write text messages,
5  Thanks to DVDs, fewer and fewer
6  The more I use my mobile phone,

a)  starting to use social networking sites.
b)  the worse our spelling becomes.
c)  the cheaper smartphones are becoming.
d)  the more I depend on it.
e)  upload music faster and faster.
f)  people go to the cinema now.

**B  Decide which sentences in Exercise A are repeated comparatives and which are double comparatives. Write the sentence numbers in the blanks.**

a)  Repeated comparatives ___ ___ ___
b)  Double comparatives ___ ___ ___

**C  Choose the correct options to complete the blog.**

# Hot Topics

Home | About | Contact

## What do you think about the digital divide?

16th September  by Tom Kinney  3 comments

I think that the digital divide is getting (1) _____. And (2) _____ the divide gets, (3) _____ it will be to overcome it. The poorest people in the world will continue to become (4) _____ and the richest people will just keep on getting (5) _____. The 'One Laptop per Child' project is aiming to close the divide by giving laptops to the world's poorest children. In my opinion, (6) _____ that all kids have access to the internet, (7) _____ the digital divide will be closed.

| | | | | |
|---|---|---|---|---|
| 1 | a) | worse and worse | b) | the worse |
| 2 | a) | bigger and bigger | b) | the bigger |
| 3 | a) | harder and harder | b) | the harder |
| 4 | a) | poorer and poorer | b) | the poorer |
| 5 | a) | richer and richer | b) | the richer |
| 6 | a) | sooner and sooner | b) | the sooner |
| 7 | a) | faster and faster | b) | the faster |

### WHAT'S RIGHT?

(X)  Multinational companies are becoming more dominant and more dominant.

(✓)  _____
_____

## 5 VOCABULARY: verbs for taking social action

**A** 🎧 06 Listen and write the words you hear.

1 _____    3 _____    5 _____    7 _____

2 _____    4 _____    6 _____    8 _____

**B** Choose the correct options to complete the sentences.

1 Thousands of people _____ in a demonstration yesterday against globalisation.
   a) participated    b) generated    c) sustained

2 We must shop locally in order to _____ small businesses.
   a) value    b) sustain    c) campaign

3 Multinational companies _____ a lot of employment worldwide.
   a) campaign    b) generate    c) participate

4 It's worth paying a bit more for products in order to _____ the local economy.
   a) generate    b) value    c) support

5 Globalisation _____ free trade between countries.
   a) campaigns    b) participates    c) promotes

6 The weekly farmers' market has really _____ the local economy.
   a) boosted    b) valued    c) participated

7 If we _____ local shops, then we should spend money there, instead of shopping online.
   a) generate    b) value    c) boost

8 The politician _____ for the trade ban to be lifted.
   a) participated    b) generated    c) campaigned

## 6 WRITING: a formal email

**A** Read this email and choose the correct formal expressions.

> **To:** Miguel Moreno    **From:** ksteinmann@globe4u.com
> **Subject:** globe4u
>
> (1) Hi Miguel! / Dear Mr Moreno,
> (2) Thanks so much for applying for / Thank you for your interest in a summer holiday job
> with globe4u. There are still opportunities to work in Haiti in June and August. (3) Just tell me /
> Could you let me know which month you would prefer?
> (4) You will be required to attend / You've got to come to a meeting with me in
> order to discuss what the work involves. There are two possible dates for this: 5th May
> at 10am, or 14th May at 3pm. Please let me know which is more convenient for you.
> (5) See you at the meeting / I look forward to meeting you.
> (6) With love / Regards,
> (7) Klaus Steinmann, Director, globe4u / Klaus

**B** This formal email contains six mistakes. Underline the mistakes and rewrite the email correctly in your notebook using language from Exercise A.

> Hi Klaus!
> Thanks so much for your email.
> I would prefer to work in June rather than August and I'm available to come in to discuss the
> work on 5th May at 10am. Just tell me if there's any preparation that I can do for the meeting?
> See you then.
> With love,
> Miguel

# SkillsStudio

**A** Read the book review and answer the question below.

### Review ▶ Sustainable Travel Scott Williams    ○ £19.99

An exciting new book by best-selling author Scott Williams, *Sustainable Travel*, is perfect for adventurous travellers with a conscience. Based on his personal experiences, the author explains how we can get the most authentic experience of different cultures while ensuring that we don't harm the environment. He also explains to us how we can make certain that the money we spend ends up in the pockets of the communities we visit, rather than going to multinational tour operators.

The reviewer thinks that the main function of this book is to explain to readers how to …

a) experience different cultures.
b) have a conscience.
c) have interesting and ethical holidays.

**B** 🎧 **07** Listen to the radio interview. Number the topics in the order that you hear them discussed.

☐ The harm that tourism can do to the environment.
☐ What an ethical tourist is.
☐ How to be an ethical tourist.
☐ The harm that tourism can do to local communities.

**C** Listen again to the radio interview and complete the mind map.

(1) _____

(2) _____

**How can tourism harm the environment?**

(1) _____

(3) _____

### Scott's radio interview

**How can tourism harm local communities?**

(1) _____

(2) _____

**How can we become ethical tourists?**

(2) _____

(3) _____

**D** Listen to the radio interview again.
Match the phrases (1–6) to their correct meanings (a–f).

1 positive/negative impact
2 carbon emissions
3 natural resources
4 tourism developments
5 excess packaging
6 waste facilities

a) materials provided by nature, such as water, that can be used by humans
b) good/bad effect
c) gases released into the air when we burn fossil fuels
d) when more materials are used to wrap something than is necessary
e) places where you can dispose of rubbish
f) areas that are built up for use by visitors

**E** Listen to the radio interview again and answer these questions.

1 An ethical tourist has _____ on any place they visit.
   a) a positive rather than negative impact
   b) a negative rather than positive impact
   c) no impact at all

2 Scott says that every day there are about _____ flights worldwide.
   a) 9300
   b) 93,000
   c) 930,000

3 Tourists destroy natural habitats by …
   a) leaving rubbish behind.
   b) playing golf.
   c) flying on planes.

4 Scott mentions the golf course to show how tourism can …
   a) destroy some of the world's most beautiful, remote areas.
   b) create jobs in an area.
   c) use up a lot of the natural resources in an area.

5 John suggests that it's unrealistic to expect tourists …
   a) to leave excess packaging at home.
   b) not to travel by plane.
   c) to ask about the ethics of their tour operator.

**F** Write an opinion essay of about 250 words in your notebook on the statement below:
*Every traveller should have a positive impact on all the places they visit.*

# UNIT 3 FAME AND FORTUNE

## 1 GRAMMAR: reported speech – modal verbs and past perfect

**A Complete the sentences with the correct form of the verbs in brackets.**

1 Oscar told us we *had to wait* (*must wait*) behind the rope to get the singer's autograph.

2 Linda explained that she _____ (*never try*) to get a celebrity's autograph before.

3 Ethan said that he _____ (*can't believe*) that he _____ (*might meet*) a real star soon.

4 Olivia told us we _____ (*must take*) a lot of photographs if we got close to a celebrity.

5 Peter said that celebrities _____ (*shouldn't charge*) money for photographs or autographs.

6 Anna admitted that she _____ (*will probably never be*) famous.

> **WHAT'S RIGHT?**
>
> ✗ She told us she must work late yesterday.
>
> ✓ _____
> _____

**B Look at the status update. Complete the message.**

**Lorenzo Vega**
15 minutes ago

Like    Comment    Share

Hi, guys! Guess what? A story about me and my company will be on the Channel 5 news this afternoon! It might help our business a lot or at least it can't hurt. Anyway, I had planned to watch it at work and I still would watch it if I could, but there's an important meeting I absolutely must attend. Can someone please record it for me? Thanks! The story should be on about 4.45 today.

Hi, Mum! Do you remember my friend Lorenzo? Well, he just told me that he (1) _____ be on the Channel 5 news today! He said the story (2) _____ help his company a lot or at least it (3) _____ hurt. Lorenzo explained that he (4) _____ to watch the story at work and he said he still (5) _____ watch it if he (6) _____, but there's a problem. He told me he (7) _____ attend an important meeting. He asked if someone (8) _____ record the story for him. I'm at work, so I can't do it. Can you help, Mum? Lorenzo said the story (9) _____ be on at 4.45 today. Thanks! Kylie

## 2 VOCABULARY: ways to become famous

**A Choose the correct options to complete the ways to become famous.**

1 She inherited a cure / fortune worth millions.

2 She broke a world record / scandal in women's football.

3 He caused a novel / scandal that embarrassed his entire family.

4 She came up with a new invention / novel that helps people save energy.

5 He's a business leader who runs a global company / record.

6 He discovered a cure / an invention for a disease.

7 She wrote a best-selling novel / record about her experiences in Africa.

**B Match the sentences (1–7) in Exercise A to the sentences (a–g) below. Write the correct number of the sentence from Exercise A.**

a) ☐ He found a plant that might stop cancer.

b) ☐ She made a car that doesn't need petrol.

c) ☐ She's scored more goals than anyone else in history.

d) ☐ Millions of people bought her book.

e) ☐ He runs an airline that flies to 51 countries.

f) ☐ He cheated on a popular quiz show.

g) ☐ Her uncle died and left her his business.

# 3 READING: for different purposes

**A** **Match the ways of reading to the definitions.**

1  skimming
2  scanning
3  reading in detail

a) reading a text carefully to learn concepts and details
b) looking quickly at a text to get a general idea of what it's about
c) looking for specific information in a text

**B** **Read the questions and answer them using an appropriate method from Exercise A. Write a, b or c to indicate which method you chose.**

1  ____ In which publication did the interview with this celebrity originally appear? _____

2  ____ What issue is this celebrity trying to tackle? _____

3  ____ What does the celebrity say the government is doing at the moment about this issue? _____

4  ____ Which celebrity is the article about? _____
5  ____ When is Food Revolution Day? _____
6  ____ Why does this famous person think it's important to teach children how to cook? _____

## The Weekly Round-up

| Home | **News** | Science | Technology | Environment | Politics | Sports |

### Jamie Oliver wants childhood obesity at the top of the political agenda

TV chef Jamie Oliver is today calling for the appointment of a "political visionary" to solve the obesity crisis engulfing the UK. He said he wanted at least one of the political parties to come up with "one pioneer, one visionary who's going to put prevention [of childhood obesity] at the heart of its campaign" for next year's election. "You can't have one arm of the Government investing money in food education and school lunches and then have another part promoting junk food, to be licensed and given permission to trade within a stone's throw of a school," he said in an interview with the Times Education Supplement published today.

The TV chef is famous for his campaign to improve school dinners during the 2005 election campaign, which led to the adoption of new healthy eating standards in schools. He said "There is not one country on the planet which has overcome the obesity crisis – not one country where obesity levels are coming down." and added that it needed "50 or 60" decisions and initiatives to happen at once followed by a five-year strategy to improve eating habits. Latest figures show almost a third of 10- and 11-year-olds and over a fifth of four- to five-year-olds are either overweight or obese. Mr Oliver added, "Governments will ask 'what is the one thing we can do?'", "But if you think [just] one thing, you're always going to lose: nothing will be achieved."

Mr Oliver was making his comments in advance of Food Revolution Day on 16th May, when he will be broadcasting a cooking class for children across the globe via his own TV channel and those of the Times Education Supplement. He will be attempting to break the Guinness World Record for the largest number of people cooking the same dish on the same day. All those who tune in will be asked to cook a "Rainbow Wrap", a coleslaw with little pieces of feta cheese wrapped in flatbread.

Mr Oliver said: "Getting kids cooking from as early as possible helps them to develop an essential life skill which will have a huge impact on their future health and wellbeing."

## 4 VOCABULARY: guessing meaning from context

**Read the sentences and choose the correct meaning of the words in bold.**

1  My savings have been **dwindling** over the last few months, a few pounds a day.
   a)  decreasing slowly      b)  decreasing rapidly

2  Many celebrities find being famous so **traumatic** that they need psychological help.
   a)  having an extremely negative effect      b)  having a slightly negative effect

3  It's troubling that more and more young children have **aspirations** to be famous.
   a)  something you want to achieve in the future      b)  something you want to do right now

4  Many celebrities who **make it big** find that having lots of money and fans still doesn't make them happy.
   a)  become rich but not famous      b)  become rich and famous

5  Being **in the spotlight** has good and bad points; one day the media praises you and the next day they criticise you.
   a)  well-known and well-loved      b)  well-known but not always well-loved

6  After three decades of fame and attention, the actor suddenly found himself **washed-up** and forgotten.
   a)  no longer famous      b)  famous as a child but not as an adult

7  Many stars are depressed when they aren't on stage and feel a deep sense of **worthlessness**.
   a)  an angry feeling      b)  a sad feeling

8  Sadly, many celebrities don't realise that **self-esteem** comes from within, not from others.
   a)  loving yourself      b)  being loved by others

## 5 GRAMMAR: reported speech – optional back-shifting

**A  Look at the sentences. If we reported each sentence with *She said*, is back-shifting O (optional) or N (necessary)? Write the correct letter.**

1  ___ 'Reality TV and celebrity gossip magazines are more popular than ever.'
2  ___ 'We'll all be famous pop stars in five years.'
3  ___ 'Those two actresses are wearing the same dress.'
4  ___ 'Jay Z is never going to be a successful rapper.'
5  ___ 'It takes talent, hard work and luck to succeed as an actor.'

**WHAT'S RIGHT?**

- ✗ They said she will never be famous but years later she became a big star.
- ✓ _____
  _____
  _____

**B  Match the sentences in Exercise A to the reasons why back-shifting is optional or necessary. Write the number of the sentence in Exercise A.**

a)  ☐ The sentence reports a general truth. Back-shifting is optional.
b)  ☐ The sentence reports something that is true right now. Back-shifting is optional.
c)  ☐ The sentence reports future possibilities or plans. Back-shifting is optional.
d)  ☐ The sentence reports something that is no longer true. Back-shifting is necessary.

**C  Rewrite the sentence in Exercise A that needs back-shifting.**

She said that _____.

**D  Read the interview. Then choose the correct options to complete the report of the interview. If both choices are possible, choose both.**

**Man:** Olivia Smart, welcome. Do you think you'll win tonight?

**Olivia:** I don't know. I'm probably not going to win but I really want this award. I'm wearing my lucky earrings!

**Man:** Why is this award so special to you?

**Olivia:** Well, every actress dreams of winning this award. You know, this business isn't easy. I remember my family told me, 'You'll never be a star in Hollywood.' But they were wrong!

**Man:** What will you do if you win?

**Olivia:** I'll probably cry a lot!

The interviewer reported his conversation: 'I've just spoken to Olivia Smart. She said **(1)** she's probably not going to win / she probably wasn't going to win but she also admitted that she really **(2)** wants / wanted this award. And she said **(3)** she's wearing / she was wearing her lucky earrings, so maybe that will help! She also told us that every actress **(4)** dreams / dreamed of winning this award and added that the entertainment business **(5)** isn't / wasn't easy. Her family told her that she **(6)** will never be / would never be a star in Hollywood, but they were wrong. Finally, Olivia predicted that she **(7)** will cry / would cry a lot if she wins the award tonight. So, will Olivia Smart be crying for joy later tonight? I guess we'll just have to wait and see.'

## 6 COMMUNICATION STRATEGY: clarifying misunderstandings

**A  Put the words in the correct order to make clarifications.**

1  meant / actually, / I / that's / what / not

   _____

2  easy, / fame / way / isn't / put / that / it

   _____

3  I'm / maybe / myself / not / making / clear

   _____

4  that / I / perhaps / rephrase / should

   _____

5  complicated / what / I / was, / meant / it's

   _____

6  it's / a problem / is, / say / to / I'm / what / trying

   _____

**B  »⟩ 08  Listen and write a–f to guess what the final part of each conversation will be.**

1 ___  2 ___  3 ___  4 ___  5 ___  6 ___

a) Well, perhaps I should rephrase that – he's one of the greatest athletes ever.

b) What I'm trying to say is, fame makes it hard for famous people to maintain relationships with non-celebrities because their lives are so different.

c) Actually, that's not what I meant. She's got some talent. She's good at promoting herself. But he's just so much more talented.

d) Talent used to come first, put it that way. In the past, kids wanted to be famous for being good at something. Now they just want fame!

e) Maybe I'm not making myself clear. I don't read horror books at all. They're too scary for me!

f) Well, what I meant was, you can come up with your own idea, like sitting in a tree for the longest time or something, and then do it, and you get famous!

**C  »⟩ 09  Listen to the complete conversations and check your answers.**

# SkillsStudio

**A Read the article about three famous Englishmen and answer the questions.**

1 Tick the people in the article who were definitely real.
- ☐ Sherlock Holmes
- ☐ Winston Churchill
- ☐ King Arthur

2 Who did most of the young people in the survey *think* were real? Tick the names.
- ☐ Sherlock Holmes
- ☐ Winston Churchill
- ☐ King Arthur

**B Read the text again. Find a synonym for each of these words in the paragraphs indicated.**

1 lack of understanding (paragraph A):

_____

2 not real (paragraph B):

_____

3 valuable object (paragraph C):

_____

4 encouraged (paragraph D):

_____

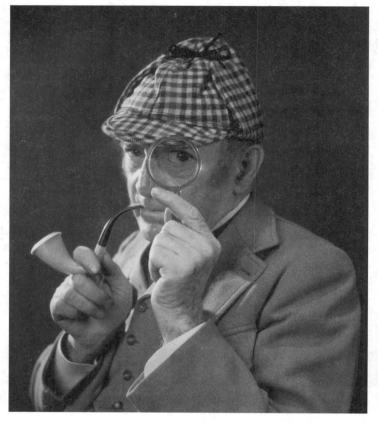

**C Read the text again and choose the correct sentence for each gap. There is one extra sentence that you do not need to use.**

a) However, some scholars say there is evidence that he really existed.
b) We shall never surrender.
c) Researchers asked 3000 people under 20 about real, historical figures and also characters from stories.
d) The books are still popular today, and some of the most famous have been made into films and TV programmes.
e) You might name John Lennon or Paul McCartney of the Beatles, or perhaps a famous athlete like David Beckham.

**D Match the two parts to make complete sentences. There are three extra options that you do not need to use.**

1 Researchers asked 3000 young people about

2 Sir Arthur Conan Doyle was

3 People around the world

4 The Knights of the Round Table were

5 Churchill gave his most famous speeches

6 Twenty per cent of British teenagers

a) send letters to Sherlock Holmes.
b) believe that Churchill wasn't real.
c) told researchers that Holmes was real.
d) in the late 1800s and early 1900s.
e) in the early 1940s.
f) real and fictional Englishmen.
g) King Arthur's trusted followers.
h) the author of the Sherlock Holmes stories.
i) Sherlock Holmes' assistant.

**E Write an opinion essay of about 250 words on the following statement:**

*It isn't important for people to know whether characters are real or not. Fictional characters can provide true inspiration, and that's all that matters.*

# *World-famous Englishmen:*
## Real or fictional?

**If you were asked to name three famous English people, who would be on your list? (1)** _____ **You might also name Sherlock Holmes, Sir Winston Churchill or even King Arthur.**

**A**   Researchers who wanted to learn more about what the UK's young people know about their own famous countrymen and women have made an interesting discovery. After surveying 3000 British people under the age of 20, researchers learned that, although young people do know the names and adventures of Holmes, Churchill and Arthur, there is confusion about which of the men are real and which are fictional characters.

**B** *Sherlock Holmes*

One of the most famous Englishmen in the world is Sherlock Holmes, a 19th century detective who, in fact, never really existed. Created by author Sir Arthur Conan Doyle, Holmes and his assistant, Dr Watson, were fictional characters who lived in London in the late 1800s and early 1900s. Holmes began working as a detective in 1887, and his fame grew quickly due to his ability to solve difficult crimes through careful observation and the use of logic. Watson wrote books telling the stories of some of the cases Holmes solved. **(2)** _____ There is even a Sherlock Holmes museum at 221b Baker Street, London, an address made famous as the house where Holmes lived and worked.

Given the detective's great fame and the fact that his fictional house can be found at a real address in London, perhaps it's not surprising that researchers found that 58% of British teenagers believed Holmes was a real person. These young British people are not alone in their confusion either. Through the years, people around the world have sent letters to Sherlock Holmes at 221b Baker Street, asking for his help.

**C** *King Arthur*

Another famous Englishman that the researchers asked about was King Arthur. Legends tell of the huge, round table where the great king sat with his most trusted knights – known, perhaps not surprisingly, as the Knights of the Round Table. But why a round table? Because at a round table, no one has the most important seat, and everyone is equal. Arthur's best-known adventure might be his search for the Holy Grail, a holy treasure. They searched for years, but unfortunately their quest ended in defeat.

According to the stories, Arthur lived in the 5th or 6th century. But was he real? In the same survey of British teenagers, 65% said he was real. The experts aren't sure, however. Many historians believe Arthur was invented by a writer in the 12th century. **(3)** _____

**D** *Sir Winston Churchill*

Researchers also asked the subjects of their survey about the British leader Winston Churchill. Churchill, born in 1874, worked in politics most of his adult life, but he is best remembered for his courage and leadership of Great Britain in the dark years of 1940–1945, during World War II. The speeches that he gave as Prime Minister inspired the British people and he will always be remembered as one of the country's toughest fighters and greatest leaders. 'We shall go on to the end,' he declared in 1940 in one of his most famous speeches. 'We shall fight on the seas and oceans, … we shall fight on the beaches, … we shall fight in the fields and in the streets, … **(4)** _____'

There are photos, recordings and film of Churchill's speeches and yet, in the survey of British teenagers, 20% said he was a fictional character.

# UNIT 4 UPS AND DOWNS

## 1 LISTENING: understanding discourse markers

**A** 🎧 **10 Listen to the podcast and choose T (true) or F (false).**

| | | |
|---|---|---|
| 1 | The happiest country in the world according to the OECD is Norway. | T / F |
| 2 | The OECD surveys people in 11 different countries. | T / F |
| 3 | Six hundred thousand people have answered the survey. | T / F |
| 4 | The most important thing to most people is life satisfaction. | T / F |
| 5 | Greece ranks 35th in the list of countries. | T / F |
| 6 | Life in Turkey has improved recently for its citizens. | T / F |

**B Listen again. Number the discourse markers (a–l) in the order that you hear them.**

a) In addition ☐
b) As a result ☐
c) In general ☐
d) On the other hand ☐
e) On the whole ☐
f) That said ☐

g) Furthermore ☐
h) As a consequence ☐
i) To a great extent ☐
j) Consequently ☐
k) Nevertheless ☐
l) What's more ☐

**C Write the letters of the discourse markers from Exercise B next to their correct function.**

1 To talk generally: ___, ___, ___
2 To introduce a contrasting point: ___, ___, ___
3 To introduce a result: ___, ___, ___
4 To introduce an additional point: ___, ___, ___

## 2 VOCABULARY: life satisfaction

**A Write the words from the box in the correct gaps below.**

appreciate   appreciation   content   contentment   enjoy   enjoyment
happiness   happy   pleasant   pleasure   satisfaction   satisfy   wealth   wealthy

**Nouns:** _____, _____, _____, _____, _____,
_____, _____

**Adjectives:** _____, _____, _____, _____

**Verbs:** _____, _____, _____

**B** Complete the sentences with a word from Exercise A.
**For some sentences more than one answer is possible.**

1 Did you _____ your trip to Spain?
2 He used to be a _____ man but he lost his fortune in the stock market crash.
3 It was with great _____ that the teacher gave her students their scores.
4 Joe is very _____ when he's away from the city.
5 We really _____ the effort that you've made for us.
6 Some people think the most important thing in life is money, but for me it's _____.
7 We were having a very _____ day until we got lost.

## 3 GRAMMAR: noun clauses as objects

**A** Replace the words in brackets with one of the words from the box.

how   what   when   where   why

1 Can you tell me (*the time that*) _____ the film starts?
2 I don't know (*the reason that*) _____ he's in such a good mood today.
3 Do you know (*the way that*) _____ he became so wealthy?
4 Tell me (*the place that*) _____ you want to meet.
5 I appreciate (*the things that*) _____ you've done for me.

**B** Choose the correct options to complete the sentences.

1 I don't understand _____ I'm feeling so happy but I'm not complaining!
   a) what      b) why      c) when
2 I feel very angry about _____ I was treated during my trip.
   a) when      b) where      c) how
3 Could you let me know _____ the best time to call would be?
   a) when      b) how      c) why
4 The students couldn't hear _____ the lecturer was saying.
   a) why      b) when      c) what
5 Do you remember _____ you were when you last saw your keys?
   a) what      b) where      c) why

**C** Complete the conversation with words from
Exercise A.

**Ann:** Hi! Do you want to come to a life skills seminar with me tonight?
**José:** Sure! Do you know (1) _____ it's about?
**Ann:** Well, the title is, 'Understanding yourself and your emotions'. So, I guess it's about (2) _____ we feel the way we do.
**José:** Cool. Did you check (3) _____ it starts? I hope it's not too late!
**Ann:** It isn't. It's at 7.15. I don't know (4) _____ it's being held, but Dave said it would probably be in the Arts Centre. I'll check, OK?
**José:** Great. Do you know (5) _____ you're getting there? Do you want to meet first and go together?
**Ann:** Sounds good!

**WHAT'S RIGHT?**

✗ I don't know where did he go.

✓ _____

## 4 VOCABULARY: mood

**A** ))🎧 **11** Listen and write the words and phrases you hear.

1 _____     5 _____
2 _____     6 _____
3 _____     7 _____
4 _____     8 _____

**B** Complete the sentences with words or phrases from Exercise A.

1 I just can't concentrate on my work today – I don't know why I'm so _____, but I need to be more _____ so that I can finish this essay.

2 Sam always sees the best in every situation because she's so _____. Her husband, Costas, is much more negative and always expects the worst – he's very _____.

3 Kao's _____ have been very up and down since he moved to the city, but he's trying to achieve a _____ so that he can look to the future and move on with his life.

4 Whenever I'm feeling low and _____, I talk to Jon because he's always _____ and he cheers me up.

## 5 GRAMMAR: review of conditional forms

**A** Complete the grammar rules.

**Zero conditional**: to talk about things that are generally true
*If* + **(1)** _____, present simple
**1st conditional**: to talk about things that are likely or possible in the future
*If* + **(2)** _____, *will* (*won't*) + base form
**2nd conditional**: to talk about things that are unreal or unlikely in the present or future
*If* + **(3)** _____, + *would*(*n't*) + base form
**3rd conditional**: to talk about unreal situations in the past
*If* + **(4)** _____, *would*(*n't*) *have* + past participle

**B** Complete the sentences with the correct forms of the verbs in brackets.

1 I've never seen the film. I _____ (*cry*) if I _____ (*watch*) it last night.

2 Denise might see Karl today. If she _____ (*see*) him, she _____ (*tell*) him your good news.

3 I'm unhappy because I don't have enough money. If I _____ (*be*) wealthy, I _____ (*be*) very happy.

4 I saw Chi today, but I didn't know he was depressed. If he _____ (*tell*) me, I _____ (*could/help*) him.

5 If you _____ (*have*) good friends, they always _____ (*help*) if you have problems.

6 If you _____ (*not/take*) this opportunity, you _____ (*regret*) it.

### WHAT'S RIGHT?

(✗) If you told me he was depressed, I would have called him.

(✓) _____
_____
_____

**C  This conversation contains six mistakes with conditional forms. Find the mistakes and correct them.**

Sian: What are you reading?

Lisa: It's an article called *The Key to Happiness*. I read you some sections if you're interested.

Sian: All right.

Lisa: OK, well, it says that if you wanted to be happy, then be a good friend, because strong relationships are the key to contentment.

Sian: I think that's true. I love spending time with my friends and if I didn't have them, I will be very unhappy.

Lisa: Me, too. It also says that people are usually more satisfied with life if they did a job that they love.

Sian: Yeah, that's true, too. Do you remember last year when I was doing that office job I hated? If I hadn't got a new job in the music store, I will still be miserable.

Lisa: Hmm, and probably the reason I'm not that happy right now is because I don't have a job I enjoy. I think if I have a job that I loved, then I would be more content.

Sian: I totally agree. So, stop reading that article and check out the job listings instead!

Lisa: Good point!

## 6 WRITING: a thank-you note

**A  Put the words in the correct order to make expressions used in thank-you notes.**

1 generous / your / so / was / donation

_____

2 express / I / for / gratitude / also / my / would / to / like

_____

3 again / of / thanks / all / us / here / from

_____

4 you / writing / I / to / for / am / thank

_____

**B  Read Cecilia's thank-you note. Complete each gap with an expression from Exercise A.**

To: Simon Barbier    From: Cecilia Harris
Re: Crowdfunding donation

Dear Mr Barbier,
(1) _____ your contribution to our Crowdfunding Project to raise money to set up a new community centre for unemployed young people. It's great that local business leaders are taking an interest in the project.
(2) _____ and has helped us on our way to achieving our final target. We are hoping to open the centre next summer and we'll keep you updated on our progress.
(3) _____ your kind offer to deliver a talk at the centre once it is up and running. I think this would be very beneficial and that our members would learn a great deal from hearing about your business experiences. I'll be in touch to arrange details at a later date.
(4) _____
Yours sincerely,
Cecilia Harris

# SkillsStudio

**A** Read the opinions and decide whether the speakers are optimistic or pessimistic.

> 1 'I'm in my early 20s, and I find it difficult to get excited about the future. There's so much unemployment in my country and I don't know if there'll be a job for me when I finish university. I find the uncertainty very hard to live with.'

☐ optimistic  ☐ pessimistic

> 2 'Well, I'm in my mid 40s now and I've never felt better. I've got over the insecurities of my early 20s, so I can really enjoy life to the full now.'

☐ optimistic  ☐ pessimistic

> 3 'I was really happy when I was in my early 20s. Then life got me down a little bit as I went through middle age, but I've come out on the other side, and now I'm in my late 60s, I'm happier than I've ever been. My body may not be as young as it used to be but the future looks bright!'

☐ optimistic  ☐ pessimistic

**B** 🎧 **12** Susie is discussing a report with her grandfather, Ron, about satisfaction levels at different stages of life. Listen once and answer these questions.

1  According to the report, what are the two ages that we feel happiest in life?

_____ , _____

2  Which speaker from Exercise A agrees with the findings of the report?

_____

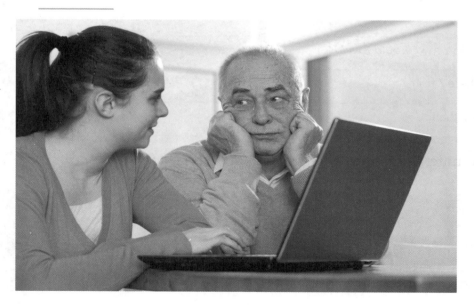

**C** Listen again and match the words and phrases you heard in the conversation (1–6) with their definitions (a–f).

| | | | |
|---|---|---|---|
| 1 | peak | a) | think something is worse or less important than it really is |
| 2 | make the most of | b) | reach its highest or greatest level |
| 3 | overestimate | c) | follow |
| 4 | underestimate | d) | think something is better or more important than it really is |
| 5 | pursue | e) | enjoy or use something as much as possible |
| 6 | generalise | f) | say something about a group of people or things that is true for most of them |

**D** Listen again and choose the correct options to complete the table.

| Age | According to report, our satisfaction levels are … | Ron's opinion of report findings |
| --- | --- | --- |
| 23 | **(1)** high / low / increasing / declining. | **(2)** He agrees / disagrees / doesn't say. |
| 30s and 40s | **(3)** high / low / increasing / declining. | **(4)** He agrees / disagrees / doesn't say. |
| Mid 50s | **(5)** high / low / increasing / declining. | **(6)** He agrees / disagrees / doesn't say. |
| After 55 | **(7)** high / low / increasing / declining. | **(8)** He agrees / disagrees / doesn't say. |
| 69 | **(9)** high / low / increasing / declining. | **(10)** He agrees / disagrees / doesn't say. |
| After 75 | **(11)** high / low / increasing / declining. | **(12)** He agrees / disagrees / doesn't say. |

**E** Listen again and choose the correct answers.

1 According to the report, 23-year-olds predict that they will be … in the future than they really will be.
   a) 10% more satisfied
   b) 10% less satisfied
   c) 10% more disappointed
   d) 10% less disappointed

2 According to the report, people in their mid 50s feel sad because they realise that …
   a) they won't be able to make the dreams of their youth a reality.
   b) they are getting older.
   c) their bodies are not able to do what they used to do.
   d) they need to have lower expectations in life.

3 When Ron was 53, he …
   a) got a new job in sales.
   b) became a yoga instructor.
   c) realised his dreams weren't going to come true.
   d) had a career change that made him more wealthy.

4 According to the report, people who are 69 …
   a) are less happy than they were when they were younger because they expect more from life.
   b) are happier than they were when they were younger because they expect less from life.
   c) are happier than they were when they were younger because they are so wise.
   d) are happier than they were when they were younger because they do yoga.

5 The report was based on data from … people.
   a) 21,161
   b) 23,151
   c) 23,161
   d) 20,161

6 They spoke to people from all over Germany and the results were … the people were from different backgrounds.
   a) exactly the same even though
   b) completely different even though
   c) completely different because
   d) almost the same even though

**F** Do you agree or disagree with the findings of the report that Susie talked about? Write an online comment of about 200 words in response to the article.

# UNIT 5 SOMETHING IN THE WATER

## 1 GRAMMAR: the passive

**A** Match each tense (1–5) to the correct form of the passive (a–e).

| | | | |
|---|---|---|---|
| 1 | present simple | a) | Beijing's Olympic pool is still being used, years after the Games. |
| 2 | past simple | b) | The original pool hadn't been designed as a water park. |
| 3 | present continuous | c) | The pool has been transformed into a water park. |
| 4 | present perfect | d) | The Olympic Games were held there in 2008. |
| 5 | past perfect | e) | It is located near the Bird's Nest Stadium. |

**B** Choose the correct options to complete the article.

### Beijing's Water Cube Transformed

When the Beijing Olympic pool **(1)** has been built / was first built, it was called The Water Cube due to its extraordinary cube-shaped exterior. Now, several years after the Olympics, the inside is just as incredible. The place where Michael Phelps **(2)** has been awarded / was awarded eight gold medals **(3)** has been transformed / is transformed into an enormous indoor water park – the largest in Asia. It already has waterslides, a wave pool and an indoor river, and new rides **(4)** were added / are being added every year. The site, which **(5)** is now called / is now being called Happy Magic Water Park, **(6)** was designed / is being designed to look like an underwater environment and is decorated with colourful jellyfish, coral and floating bubbles. Unlike sites in other Olympic cities, the Water Cube **(7)** hasn't been abandoned / hadn't been abandoned for long before it **(8)** was redesigned / had been redesigned, so the transformation was not difficult. Since it opened, the park **(9)** was visited / has been visited by more than two million people and it is the second most popular tourist spot in China, after the Great Wall. Beijing residents say they are glad this wonderful building **(10)** has still been used / is still being used and enjoyed by so many people.

### WHAT'S RIGHT?

ⓧ Dozens of homes were damaging by the flood.

✓ _____

**C** Complete the email with the correct form of the passive. Use the verbs and words in brackets.

**To:** Igor    **From:** Aliyu
**Subject:** Hi from Jordan!

Hi, Igor! Greetings from the hot springs in Jordan! This place is so cool. It **(1)** _____ (*locate*) in an oasis near the Dead Sea. Even though we're in the middle of the desert, there is a lot of water here. The water comes from a small desert river, as well as from several hot spring waterfalls. The spa **(2)** _____ (*build*) a few years ago because people say the warm, salty water is good for your health. This afternoon, I **(3)** _____ (*give*) a two-hour Six Senses massage with warm water and mud from the sea. It felt so therapeutic!
The spa is beautiful and they're making changes to it all the time. Right now, the walls inside the hotel **(4)** _____ (*paint*) in natural colours, and my room **(5)** _____ (*recently/decorate*). It's like an Arabian palace! Yesterday morning, I lay by the pool in the canyon. Then I had an incredible lunch on the terrace, overlooking the waterfalls. An organic vegetable garden **(6)** _____ (*recently/plant*) in the grounds, so fresh vegetables **(7)** _____ (*always/serve*) in the restaurants. Unfortunately, I fell asleep after that and missed dinner. It was supposed to be a special 'Bedouin-style' meal by candlelight in the olive grove, but when I got there all the food **(8)** _____ (*clear away*)! I'll upload some pictures for you to look at soon. Take care, Aliyu

## 2 READING: inferring opinion

**A  Read about three hotels. Write the letter of the paragraph heading (a, b or c) next to the name of the hotel.**

**a)**  Pamper yourself in a glamorous getaway

**b)**  Spend the night in a hotel made of frozen water

**c)**  Head to the bottom of the sea for a unique experience

## *The best hotels* on (and under!) the water

Everyone loves to take a holiday by the sea, but for some travellers, even a five-star beach resort isn't enough. If you're one of those tourists, you might give these hotels a try.

**1  Jules' Underwater Lodge:** ___
Originally a research lab, the lodge is set entirely under water at the bottom of a lagoon in Florida. Guests wishing to stay there have to scuba dive 6.5 metres below the surface of the water – those not able to scuba dive are required to take a short course first. The lodge has the kind of comforts you'd expect to see in any hotel, such as hot showers, phones, TVs and a well-stocked kitchen. But what **(1)** <u>sets it apart</u> is the view of the rich and varied marine life swimming past the windows. **(2)** <u>For the lucky few who get to stay there</u>, it's this view that has the most profound effect. Many describe the experience as the most incredible of their lives.

**2  The Burj Al-Arab Hotel:** ___
In the pristine waters of the Arabian Gulf stands the Hotel Burj Al-Arab. The world's first seven-star hotel, opened for the Millennium, has been designed like a ship's sail. Here you can find 202 luxurious suites, infinity pools, chauffeured shopping, personal butlers, helicopter tours … **(3)** <u>And that's just the beginning</u> … Don't forget to visit the underwater restaurant – accessed by a submarine – and enjoy your dinner in the company of sharks. If **(4)** <u>that's not your cup of tea</u>, be sure to visit the Burj Al-Arab's upstairs restaurant one evening, if only to admire the view. Gaze over the Arabian Gulf and the extraordinary man-made Palm Islands below.

**3  Hôtel de Glace:** ___
If you want to stay on the water, this hotel near Quebec City in Canada offers **(5)** <u>a unique twist</u>: the entire hotel is made of ice. Hôtel de Glace is French for 'Ice Hotel', and it is open only during the winter months. The café, bar and restaurant are all made of ice, as are the tables, chairs and beds. The rooms have beautiful ice sculptures and, for those **(6)** <u>who have had their fill of</u> frozen things, fireplaces. For obvious reasons, the fireplaces are not made of ice.

**B  Read the texts in Exercise A again. Choose the best definition for the underlined phrases.**

1  **a)**  makes it special                                   **b)**  puts it a long distance away
2  **a)**  a few people who stay there have good fortune        **b)**  not many people have the opportunity to stay there
3  **a)**  the hotel offers much more than this                 **b)**  the end of your stay is different
4  **a)**  you want a hot drink                                 **b)**  you don't like that kind of thing
5  **a)**  an interesting variation                             **b)**  a hotel that rotates
6  **a)**  who do not want any more                             **b)**  who really enjoy

## 3 VOCABULARY: marketing

**A** 🎧 **13** Listen to the conversation in a restaurant. Why doesn't the woman want to order bottled water?

a) It costs too much.   b) It's bad for the environment.   c) both of these reasons

**B** Listen again. Put the phrases related to marketing in the order that you hear them (1–5).

- ☐ range from … to …
- ☐ market … as …
- ☐ to make … worth …
- ☐ put up against …
- ☐ as much about … as …

**C** Complete the contribution to the online debate using the words from Exercise B.

LOGIN

| HOME | FORUMS | PROFILE | ABOUT |

**enviroKING**
Join date: 16/11
Location: Malta
Posts: 2091

31ˢᵗ July 11.53am

Given the lack of water on this planet, I think the price of bottled water is not high enough! Where I live, the price of a bottle of water usually **(1)** _____ €2.00 _____ €3.50. That's nothing to people here. Even worse, companies **(2)** _____ bottled water _____ something you buy to use the contents and then throw away the packaging. So people waste water and pollute the environment with plastic rubbish. People need to think twice before buying bottled water. As consumers, our choices should be **(3)** _____ helping the planet _____ our own convenience.

**Jenny497**
Join date: 08/01
Location: London
Posts: 147

31ˢᵗ July 12.08pm

I agree with you to a certain extent. We should conserve water and reduce rubbish. But is bottled water too cheap? No way! Companies are selling it for £5, £6, even £10 a bottle now. When you **(4)** _____ bottled water _____ other products like milk or even petrol, it's actually extremely expensive. **(5)** _____ a simple bottle of water _____ that kind of money, the bottle would have to be made of gold! People should just buy a reusable bottle and refill it with water from home.

## 4 COMMUNICATION STRATEGY: suggesting alternatives

**A** Choose the correct expressions to complete the text.

**Sadia:** Look at this. What can we do to raise awareness about water pollution?

**Tom:** We could try **(1)** collecting / collect some rubbish from the river and displaying it.

**Sadia:** I like that idea! I'd suggest **(2)** to put / putting it on display by the river.

**Tom:** Maybe, but the rubbish might fall into the river again. What about **(3)** display / displaying it somewhere indoors? There **(4)** is / was always the school.

**Jess:** No, not the school. Since adult shoppers throw most of the rubbish in the river, let's focus on them. Have you considered **(5)** give / giving the shopping centre a try?

**Tom:** Nice idea, but I don't think it would accept the rubbish. Hey, what if we **(6)** take / taking photos of the rubbish instead? We could display photos in the shopping centre.

**Jess:** Or another option would be to **(7)** hand / handing out leaflets …

**B** 🎧 **14** Listen to the conversation and check your answers.

**Stop water pollution**

**Help us rais  awareness.**

## 5 GRAMMAR: expressions of purpose

**A** Complete the structures with the words and phrases from the box.

> gerund   base form   (pro)noun + clause

1. for + _____
2. in order (not) to + _____
3. so as (not) to + _____
4. so (that) + _____
5. to + _____

**B** Complete the facts about water using the structures in Exercise A. More than one answer is possible in some cases.

### WHAT'S RIGHT?

Ⓧ Everyone must drink water for stay healthy.

✓ _____

## Water facts

Water is important (1) _____ transporting nutrients around your body. It is also needed for good digestion, circulation and temperature control, among other functions. Lack of water can cause headaches, poor concentration and many other issues. That's why it's important to drink enough water and stay hydrated. Experts say that you need to drink about eight cups of water every day. Here are a few tips for getting enough water every day:

Eating fruit is ideal (2) _____ help you receive your eight cups, and soup is also great (3) _____ including more liquids in your diet.

(4) _____ be healthy, avoid drinking too much caffeine. Drink plain water or herbal infusions. When you feel thirsty, your body has already lost 1% of its total water.

Drink water throughout exercise (5) _____ you don't dehydrate.

Be careful in hot weather. (6) _____ become dehydrated, drink water every hour – even if you don't feel thirsty.

## 6 VOCABULARY: environmental issues

**A** Put the letters into the correct order to make words and phrases.

1. rawet nulloptio _____
2. namefi _____
3. neeghiy _____
4. odflo _____
5. trawe trovepy _____
6. grudtho _____
7. essadie _____
8. limecat enchag _____

**B** Complete the text using the correct form of the words from Exercise A.

Mama Mbaga does not suffer from economic poverty, but she experiences (1) _____ on a daily basis. Without tap water, the closest source of water is a well. 'Pesticides have been stored in nearby huts for years,' she says, 'and now the wells have been polluted.' Serious (2) _____ is the result. A second problem, she says, is that 'many locals have never been taught about (3) _____, so they reuse the same water for everything. Sadly, people catch (4) _____ and die from the dirty water. In order to avoid this, we have to boil water.' The third problem, she explains, is new: 'We've always had a rainy season and a dry season, but (5) _____ means that these seasons are more extreme.' Now they suffer from excessive rains and even serious (6) _____ during the rainy season, and during the dry season the climate is so dry they experience (7) _____. 'We are not hungry yet, but who knows what's next? Perhaps a (8) _____.'

# SkillsStudio

**A  Read the article and choose the best title.**

1  Check out your water footprint!
2  Water footprinting – a new approach to water conservation
3  Global water poverty continues to grow

**B  Choose the correct definition of a water footprint.**

1  A measurement of water volume consumed and/or polluted per item of food
2  The total volume of fresh water used to produce goods and services
3  A geographical indicator to indicate where water was used to produce items

**C  Read the article again. Underline the sentence that expresses the main idea in each paragraph.**

**D  Read the text again and answer these questions.**

1  The phrase *as a consequence* in paragraph 1 means …
   a)  however
   b)  similarly
   c)  because of this
   d)  in spite of

2  In the second paragraph, the author suggests that people don't realise that …
   a)  global warming also causes water poverty.
   b)  the issue of water resources is as important as global warming.
   c)  manufacturers are wasting water in order to reduce their carbon footprints.
   d)  the World Bank is more concerned with water poverty than global warming.

3  Which of the following is an example of the indirect use of water?
   a)  eating fruit
   b)  washing your car
   c)  using less hot water in the shower
   d)  drinking water

4  If something is *scarce* (paragraph 4), this means …
   a)  it is not used efficiently.
   b)  people only use it indirectly.
   c)  there is not very much of it.
   d)  it is bad for the environment.

5  The phrase *per capita* (paragraph 5) probably means …
   a)  for each person.
   b)  annually.
   c)  indirectly.
   d)  inside its borders.

**E  Write a blog post of about 200 words summarising the concept of the water footprint.**

# ENVIRONMENT

[1] Over the last decade, international attention has been focused on global warming and climate change. As a consequence, most of us know the concept of the carbon footprint. In simple terms, the carbon footprint shows how much $CO_2$ is created by an individual, organisation or process. Today, many businesses and organisations calculate their carbon footprints and try to reduce the amount of $CO_2$ they produce. Responsible consumers also calculate their personal carbon footprints. They then use this number to make better choices about the products they buy, the food they eat and the way they travel.

[2] There is, however, another global environmental issue that requires urgent international attention: water resources. Our planet has a limited amount of fresh water for drinking, hygiene, manufacturing and farming. One of the main problems associated with this issue is water poverty: many people do not have enough clean water for their basic needs. The World Bank has estimated that more than 700 million people in 43 countries are currently regularly affected by water poverty.

[3] As a way of drawing society's attention to the nature and scale of the problem, scientists have developed the concept of the 'water footprint'. In the same way that a carbon footprint shows how much pollution an individual, organisation or process is responsible for, the water footprint shows how much water an individual, organisation or process uses. The water footprint is calculated by adding two numbers: direct use and indirect use. The first part of the water footprint, direct use, is the water that we get directly from our taps for drinking, cooking and washing. Indirect use refers to the water used in the process of growing food and manufacturing the goods we buy such as paper, clothing and so on. The water we use indirectly is known as 'virtual water', and it is this water that is of increasing concern. However, most people do not realise or think about the amount of water they use indirectly. For this reason, the idea of the water footprint is an important way to help people realise that their choices can have an impact on water poverty. It can also show people that small changes in lifestyle can make a difference.

[4] Like carbon footprints, water footprints allow us to calculate our consumption, either as individuals or as businesses. But water footprints have a wider variety of uses than carbon footprints. Water footprints can be calculated for specific goods and products. For example, we know that it takes 15,000 litres of water to produce a kilogram of beef and 2400 for a hamburger. A cotton T-shirt requires 2000 litres. In other words, when we import a T-shirt or eat a burger made from imported beef, we may be indirectly importing water from a region where water is already scarce. Water footprints can also help consumers make choices that are better for the planet's water. For example, a vegetarian soy burger has a much smaller water footprint than the beef burger (160 litres, compared to 2400).

[5] Water footprints have also been calculated for each nation, with the result that we can compare international water consumption. The virtual water league table shows that the US is the biggest offender, with a water footprint of almost 2500 cubic metres per year per capita, while Britain's water footprint is close to the global average of 1243 cubic metres per year per capita. At 1380 cubic metres per year per person, Japan's water footprint is relatively small; however, about 77% of that amount is from indirect use outside the country, meaning water consumed in producing the products imported by Japan. In comparison, about 20% of the United States' water footprint is used outside American borders. The creators of the water footprint hope that these numbers will create awareness and stimulate international debate about ways that nations can use water more wisely.

Information source: www.waterfootprint.org

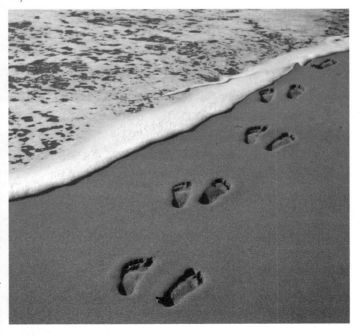

# UNIT 6 LIVING TRADITIONS

## 1 GRAMMAR: *be used to / get used to*

**A** Choose the correct options to complete the sentences.

1 I've been living next door to the airport for three years, so I 'm used to / 'm getting used to the noise now. I don't even notice it anymore.

2 I don't think I'll ever be used to / get used to commuting for three hours each day. I don't like it and never will.

3 At first, the students didn't like the new tutor but eventually they were used to / got used to him.

4 When I first moved to France, it took me a while to be used to / get used to driving on the right but now it's fine.

5 Miranda was shocked because she wasn't used to / didn't get used to being told what to do.

6 It took me a while but I eventually was used to / got used to the sound of the waves.

**B** Complete the conversation with the correct form of *be used to* or *get used to*.

Kay: Hi Jim. How are you settling in?

Jim: Pretty well, thanks. It's very different from my old job where there were only eight of us in the company, but I (1) _____ being part of a large organisation slowly.

Kay: Hmm, whenever you start a new job, it always takes a while (2) _____ a different working environment. And how are you finding living in China? Moving here must have been a big culture shock.

Jim: No, not at all. I did my training here, so I (3) _____ the local customs and I (4) _____ the language as well, because my wife is Chinese.

Kay: That must make a big difference. I know that when I first arrived here, it took me a while (5) _____ Chinese business etiquette. It's very different from the way we do business in the UK.

Jim: That's true, but no, I (6) _____ working with Chinese people, so it's been easy for me to fit in.

**WHAT'S RIGHT?**

Ⓧ I'm used to travel for my job.

Ⓥ _____

## 2 LISTENING: for main ideas

**A** Read the description of the podcast and answer the questions.

**searchallpodcasts**

SEARCH

HOME

CATEGORIES

NEWEST

RECOMMENDED

MOST POPULAR

**Love and marriage in the 21st century (11th May, 8.00pm)**

Is there still a place in today's society for weddings? Are they an important tradition or an outdated ritual? In this podcast, host Elsa Rains tries to gauge public opinion by talking to people of various ages and backgrounds. Her findings may surprise you. Download, listen and find out more.

**25 mins** [Download 15MB]

PLAY ▶  DOWNLOAD ⬇  PLAYLIST ♫  SHARE ✐

1 The main purpose of this podcast is to …
   a) give advice to people who are getting married.
   b) question the role of weddings today.

2 In the podcast, we will probably hear …
   a) a lot of different people sharing their ideas.
   b) just the host Elsa Rains sharing her ideas.

3 We may hear vocabulary such as …
   a) wedding dress, tiara, wedding cake, first dance and best man's speech.
   b) important, traditional, choice, thousands of pounds and occasion.

**B** 🎧 **15** Listen to the interviews from the podcast.
**Match each speaker to the main idea they express.**

Speaker 1     **a)**   Weddings are an unnecessary expense for the couple and their guests.

Speaker 2     **b)**   Young people today have more important things to spend their money on.

Speaker 3     **c)**   Modern weddings are more flexible than traditional weddings.

Speaker 4     **d)**   Weddings are a necessary and exciting ritual.

## 3 VOCABULARY: institutional traditions

**A** 🎧 **16** **Listen and write the words you hear.**

1 _____     3 _____     5 _____

2 _____     4 _____     6 _____

**B** **Match the words from Exercise A to their synonyms.**

1   ceremony, rite (*n.*): _____     4   first-year student (*n.*): _____

2   introduction, induction (*n.*): _____     5   good-luck symbol (*n.*): _____

3   representative (*adj.*): _____     6   upper-level (*adj.*): _____

**C** **Complete the text with words from Exercise A in the correct form.**

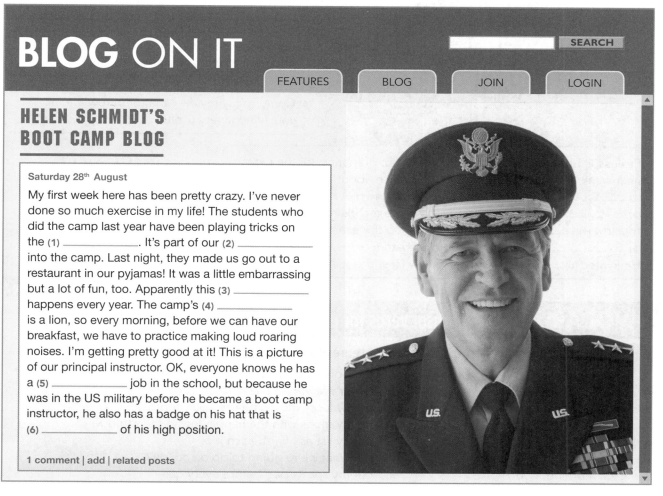

**BLOG** ON IT

SEARCH

FEATURES     BLOG     JOIN     LOGIN

### HELEN SCHMIDT'S BOOT CAMP BLOG

**Saturday 28ᵗʰ August**

My first week here has been pretty crazy. I've never done so much exercise in my life! The students who did the camp last year have been playing tricks on the **(1)** _____. It's part of our **(2)** _____ into the camp. Last night, they made us go out to a restaurant in our pyjamas! It was a little embarrassing but a lot of fun, too. Apparently this **(3)** _____ happens every year. The camp's **(4)** _____ is a lion, so every morning, before we can have our breakfast, we have to practice making loud roaring noises. I'm getting pretty good at it! This is a picture of our principal instructor. OK, everyone knows he has a **(5)** _____ job in the school, but because he was in the US military before he became a boot camp instructor, he also has a badge on his hat that is **(6)** _____ of his high position.

1 comment | add | related posts

## 4 GRAMMAR: verb + object + infinitive

**A** Put the words in the correct order to make sentences.

1 party / did / invite / he / to / you / his graduation / to / go

_____

2 for / late / to / morning / you / be / not / exercises / advise / I

_____

3 the students / be / ordered / the principal / quiet / to

_____

4 arrive / the ceremony / expect / to / they / the freshers / on / for / time

_____

**B** Read the teacher's advice and complete the text below.

> **(1)** I don't think you should worry too much about your exam next week.

> **(2)** I think it would be a really good idea if you reviewed Chapter 8 of the textbook.

> **(3)** Try to make sure that you get a good night's sleep the night before.

> **(4)** I will let you use dictionaries during the exam.

> **(5)** Remember that you must not bring mobile phones into the exam or you will fail.

> **(6)** Come to my review class tomorrow! I think you'll find it very useful!

Professor Turner gave us some advice about preparing for the exam next week. He told **(1)** _____ too much about it. He advised **(2)** _____ Chapter 8 of the textbook and he encouraged **(3)** _____ a good night's sleep before the exam. He's going to allow **(4)** _____ dictionaries during the exam, but he warned **(5)** _____ mobile phones into the exam or we would fail. He invited **(6)** _____ to his review class the following day.

### WHAT'S RIGHT?

ⓧ They even ask us don't work too hard.

✓ _____
_____
_____

## 5 VOCABULARY: phrasal verbs for personal rituals

**A** Match the two parts to make complete sentences.

1 I cross things
2 I always line
3 Before we leave, we always plan
4 I always put
5 I always clean
6 I always write
7 Each morning, I go
8 I go

a) through my bag each night to check I haven't lost anything.
b) down everything I have to do each day.
c) on my lucky gloves before I play football.
d) up my mugs with the handle facing the same way.
e) off my list as I finish each job.
f) out what we're going to do on holiday.
g) out my sports bag before every game.
h) over things I have to do that day.

**B** Complete the text with the correct form of the phrasal verbs from Exercise A.

I have a lot of personal rituals. Every night, I (1) _____ my wardrobe and (2) _____ what I'm going to wear the next day. Then when I'm getting dressed in the morning, I always have to (3) _____ my socks first – I don't know why, but it's just what I do!

Also, I work from home, so in order to stay focused, I start each day by (4) _____ a list of things that I have to do that day. I feel a real sense of achievement when I (5) _____ the list at the end of the day and (6) _____ all the items I've managed to finish.

I'm also pretty neat – while I'm working, I usually (7) _____ my pens and pencils on my desk so that they are in a straight line. Sometimes I don't even notice that I'm doing it! And I can't bear a messy desk either – I have to (8) _____ my desk drawers at least once a week!

## 6 WRITING: avoiding run-on sentences

**A** Read this instant chat. Underline the run-on sentence in each post.

| Earlier messages: | 1 day | 1 week | 2 weeks | 1 month | 3 months | 6 months | 1 year | All |

**Sarah says:** 10.58
I just returned from a walk in the woods, every New Year's Day I put on my walking boots and walk in the same place. I do this to think about the year that's passed and to make plans for the year ahead.

**Joel says:** 10.59
When my dog died, I planted a tree in the local park where we used to walk. I like it, it means I go back there every year on the anniversary of his death and remember him.

**Gabriela says:** 11.02
I have a personal ritual for when I'm worried, I buy a balloon. Then I write down my problem, tie it on the balloon and let it go. As it goes into the sky, I allow it to take away my worries and cares.

**Anna says:** 11.03
When someone I love has a problem, I write them a letter. This reminds them that I'm thinking about them, it reminds them that they aren't going through life alone.

**Spiros says:** 11.05
I made an important promise ten years ago. Now, every morning, I remember my promise, I put on my ring. (It's my wedding ring!)

**Edna says:** 11.06
I loved reading this! There are some wonderful ideas here. I don't have any rituals, now I'll try to start one.

**B** Rewrite each run-on sentence in Exercise A using a word or a punctuation mark from the box. Use each item only once.

| and | because | but | when | . | ; |

1 Sarah: _____
2 Joel: _____
3 Gabriela: _____
4 Anna: _____
5 Spiros: _____
6 Edna: _____

# SkillsStudio

**A** 🎧 **17** You will hear five short extracts in which people are talking about festivals in their country. Which festival is each speaker describing? Listen and match each photograph to the correct speaker number.

**A** ☐

**B** ☐

**C** ☐

**D** ☐

**E** ☐

**B** Listen again and match the verbs and phrasal verbs that you heard (1–8) to their definitions (a–h).

| | | | |
|---|---|---|---|
| 1 | date back | a) | make something stay the same |
| 2 | honour | b) | throw |
| 3 | boost | c) | attract |
| 4 | pull in | d) | began at a particular time in the past |
| 5 | maintain | e) | arrive |
| 6 | turn up | f) | help something to become more successful |
| 7 | hurl | g) | make, create |
| 8 | generate | h) | have respect for something |

**C** Listen again. What does each speaker say about their festival? Write the correct letter next to each speaker. There are three extra letters that you do not need to use.

a) A festival held to honour an area's local industry

b) A festival you have to pay to attend

c) A relatively modern festival to draw visitors to the area

d) A festival to celebrate the historical importance of an animal

e) A ritual based on an ancient saying

f) A festival to mark the end of winter

g) A festival to promote marine conservation

h) A ritual whose origins are not certain

Speaker 1 ____

Speaker 2 ____

Speaker 3 ____

Speaker 4 ____

Speaker 5 ____

**D** Listen again and complete the table.

| Speaker | Festival name | Country | Summary of how the festival is celebrated |
|---|---|---|---|
| 1 | | | |
| 2 | | | |
| 3 | | | |
| 4 | | | |
| 5 | | | |

**E** Write a short description of about 250 words in your notebook about a ritual or festival that takes place in your country.

# UNIT 7   DESIGNED TO PLEASE

## 1 VOCABULARY: design

**A** Put the letters into the correct order to make design words.

1   pot-yauliqt _____
2   peatmelt _____
3   unremuacaft _____
4   retaminui _____

5   quiune _____
6   envainitov _____
7   baforfalde _____
8   desporsaline _____

**B** Complete the text with the words from Exercise A.

### LEARN PRODUCT DESIGN

Are you an inventor? Do you have a **(1)** _____ idea for a product: something that no one else has thought of before?

City Design College is offering a new course in product design. As part of the coursework, you'll learn how to turn ideas into real products using the **(2)** _____ new technology of 3D printing. You'll learn how to turn your drawings into a digital **(3)** _____ that can be used to print a **(4)** _____ model of your invention. The course will also teach you how to find factories abroad that can **(5)** _____ your product. Whether you want to make **(6)** _____ kitchen tools that will sell for a few pounds, or **(7)** _____ electronic devices that will sell for thousands, this course can help you get started. Our course is **(8)** _____ so that you are learning only the things you need to know, at a pace that is best for you.

## 2 GRAMMAR: possessive apostrophe

**A** Match each use of the possessive apostrophe with an example.

1   with a singular noun

2   with a plural noun

3   to show separate ownership

4   to show joint ownership

5   with two consecutive nouns

6   with a gerund

a)   Viviane's and Tom's fashion shows were both at 8 last night.

b)   Joe and Jenny's mother helped fund their first fashion collection.

c)   Mark's design won first prize in a competition.

d)   It was Colone's daughter's idea to make an all-pink collection.

e)   The new collection's unveiling was the most exciting event of the year.

f)   It was the fashion editors' favourite collection but it sold poorly in stores.

**B** Choose the correct options to complete the sentences.

1   Dolce and Gabbana's / Dolce's and Gabbana's new collection might be the company's best ever.
2   It's terrible that designers use pink for girl's / girls' clothes and blue for boy's / boys' clothes.
3   The company closing's / company's closing will leave dozens of designers unemployed.
4   The company was named by combining the two designers' mothers' / designer's mothers' last names.
5   The designer and CEO's / designer's and CEO's ideas for the company often conflicted with each other.

### WHAT'S RIGHT?

(✗)  He designs affordable, comfortable childrens' clothes.

(✓)  _____
   _____

**C** Complete the text. Write an apostrophe (') or 's after the words. If nothing is needed, write X.

> **I had a billion-pound idea!**
> POSTED, Tuesday, 11.24pm
>
> Tonight I was looking at celebrity pictures online and thought to myself, 'I love that **(1)** star_____ shoes! Where can I get them?' Well, why isn't there a website for that? You should be able to click on **(2)** celebrities_____ **(3)** shoes_____ in a picture to find out where to buy them. My **(4)** sister_____ **(5)** husband_____ cousin is a computer programmer – maybe she can help me. She could handle the **(6)** site_____ programming, and I could do the design and talk to the shoe **(7)** companies_____. It's a great idea, isn't it? Everyone would like it – men and women, people who like **(8)** trainers_____ and people who like high **(9)** heels_____. I'm sure **(10)** Adidas_____ and **(11)** Gucci_____ marketing departments would both love it. Just remember that it's my idea – don't try to steal it!

## 3 READING: inferring factual information

**A** Read the text. Tick the statements that you can infer from the text.

1. ☐ The average person does not enjoy painting their home.
2. ☐ Only an expert can paint a room correctly.
3. ☐ Even a small amount of yellow paint can make some people angry.
4. ☐ Yellow would not be a good colour for a baby's room.
5. ☐ People may sleep better in a blue room.
6. ☐ Red is a great colour for rooms that host parties and big dinners.
7. ☐ It's a good idea to paint your bedroom red.
8. ☐ Green is a cheerful and relaxing colour.

**B** Underline the words in the text that helped you infer the ticked sentences in Exercise A.

### *Interior design pro tips:* Get in the right mood with the right colour

¹ If you're like most people, the thought of painting the walls doesn't exactly fill your heart with happiness and joy. But after the paint has dried, you want your new room to put you and your family in the right mood: cheerful in the kitchen, calm and relaxed in the bedroom and ready to party in the living room. Experts say that the colour you choose for your walls can have a real effect on the way you feel when you're in the room, so choose wisely. Here's a look at how different colours can affect your mood.

² **Yellow:** This is a cheerful colour that reminds people of sunshine. If you want to feel energised, this is a great colour for you, and is an excellent choice for dining rooms, bathrooms and kitchens. However, a little yellow goes a long way. Large amounts of yellow can make people angry. Also, according to research, babies cry more in yellow rooms.

³ **Blue:** Studies show that blue interiors can lower blood pressure and reduce your heart rate. For this reason, many people choose this relaxing colour for their bedrooms. It's also great for living rooms and other places where you want to feel calm and serene.

Lighter shades of blue are best if this is the effect you want, as dark blue can actually make people feel depressed. However, light blue can also be quite a cold colour, so make sure you add warmth to the room with furniture and fabrics.

⁴ **Red:** Red is a great choice if you want to create an exciting atmosphere and get people talking. This colour can make your heart beat faster, especially at night, and is great for living rooms and dining rooms. However, some people find it difficult to sleep well in a red room – something to remember when choosing colours for the bedroom.

⁵ **Green:** This colour brings together the best qualities of blue and yellow. You can paint nearly any room in the house green: kitchens, living rooms and bedrooms. According to studies, people often feel more comfortable and less stressed in a green interior.

⁶ **Orange:** This colour gets people excited and energised. For this reason, experts say that this is a great colour for an exercise room but it is not recommended for living rooms or bedrooms.

## 4 VOCABULARY: phrasal verbs

**A** Complete the sentences with the words from the box.

off  on  out  to  up  with

1 Is Victoria Beckham going to bring _____ a new collection this year?
2 When did Frank Gehry's career in architecture really take _____?
3 How did Jony Ive come up _____ the design for the iPod?
4 Does Zaha Hadid draw _____ her building designs herself?
5 Why do you think Prabal Gurung's designs have caught _____?
6 Do you think kids look up _____ designers?

**B** Choose the correct options to complete the article.

### Jonathan Ive

Sir Jonathan Paul 'Jony' Ive is an English designer and a top employee at Apple, Inc. When Apple first **(1)** brought out / drew up the iPod in 2001, many people gave credit to company founder Steve Jobs for **(2)** looking up to / coming up with the idea for the innovative device. However, it was Ive who **(3)** drew up / took off the first sketches of the music player. The iPod quickly **(4)** caught on / brought out with consumers, and Ive's career really **(5)** caught on / took off. Apple's success continued with the iPhone and iPad, both of which were designed by Ive. Young designers around the world **(6)** come up with / look up to Ive and he has received many awards. In 2004, the BBC named him the 'Most Influential Person in British Culture' and in 2012 he was knighted by Princess Anne.

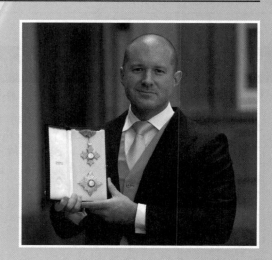

## 5 GRAMMAR: past perfect vs past perfect continuous

**A** Complete each sentence with the past perfect or past perfect continuous form of the verbs from the box. Sometimes both verb forms are possible.

be  come up with  draw up  end  open  wait

1 Because we were an hour late, the fashion show for the label's Autumn/Winter 2015 collection _____ before we arrived.
2 I _____ sample designs for two hours when the client finally turned up.
3 His design talent was clear from a young age. By the time he was 30, he _____ stores in Paris, London and Tokyo.
4 Jorge _____ in New York City for a year when he met Mika during an interior design class.
5 We _____ for over an hour before the models and designers finally arrived.
6 Maria and Jim _____ design ideas for over a year before they decided to start their own company.

### WHAT'S RIGHT?

ⓧ She didn't show anyone her designs until she had been finishing them.

✓ _____

**B** Complete the text with the past perfect or past perfect continuous form of the verbs from the box. Sometimes both forms are possible.

ask   attend   change   make   notice   think

# The first automobile designer

When Harley Earl was born in 1893, his father owned a company called the Earl Carriage Works, which (1) _____ horse-drawn carriages for several years. By 1908, the company was making parts and accessories for cars and Earl's father (2) _____ the name of his company to Earl Automobile Works. Harley Earl began studying engineering at Stanford University, but he (3) _____ classes for only a short time when he decided to work for his father instead. He began designing cars and by 1926, the general manager of General Motors (4) _____ the Earls' designs and (5) _____ him to come to Detroit to design a new Cadillac. It was so successful that Earl was asked to become head of a new department called 'the art and colour section'. This department produced some of the classic American cars of the 1950s, with fins and chrome. Earl is credited as the first designer to think of a car as a 'concept' and a car design as a work of art. Before Harley, car designers (6) _____ very little about these things.

## 6 COMMUNICATION STRATEGY: distancing language

**A** Complete the conversation with the phrases from the box.

I wanted to suggest   I was hoping   I was thinking we   I was wondering

Jim:   I want to paint the kitchen and (1) _____ we could talk about the colours.

Nick:   OK. (2) _____ might choose a neutral colour, like cream.

Jim:   Oh, really? (3) _____ using something more exciting.

Nick:   More exciting? Like what?

Jim:   (4) _____ if we should paint it orange and red.

Nick:   Orange and red?! I'm not sure that's the best idea. Those colours don't really work with the table and chairs.

Jim:   Oh, I see what you mean. Maybe cream is best, after all.

**B**   »🎧18 Listen and check your answers.

**C** Use the prompts to write requests and suggestions. Use distancing language.

1   I want / ask your opinion about / paint the bathroom blue.

_____

2   I think / we should buy a new rug / match the colour of the sofa.

_____

3   I hope my mother / help us / by come up with an idea of how to decorate the baby's room.

_____

4   I wonder / if Maria had any suggestions for an interesting design for the kitchen.

_____

# SkillsStudio

**A  Read the newspaper article about a skyscraper in London. What is the purpose of the article?**

a)  to amuse readers with stories about the building's problems
b)  to explain the mistakes in the building's design in detail
c)  to allow the building's supporters and its critics to give their opinions
d)  to propose a solution to the problems caused by the building

**B  Read the article again. Look at the words in bold and try to figure out what they mean. Then write the words from the box next to their definitions.**

| awning   context   dispute   gawk   glare   overcast   ray   scorch   spire   suspend |

1  _____ : to look at something for a long time, usually in surprise
2  _____ : a serious disagreement that lasts for a long time
3  _____ : a narrow line of light from the sun or a lamp
4  _____ : the general situation in which something happens, which helps to explain it
5  _____ : with a sky completely full of clouds
6  _____ : the pointed top of a church tower or other building
7  _____ : cloth hung above a window or door to protect against rain or sun
8  _____ : an unpleasant bright light
9  _____ : to officially stop something for a short time
10  _____ : to burn something enough to damage it

**C  Read the article again. Write the number of the paragraph that …**

a)  ☐ gives the writer's personal experience with the building.
b)  ☐ says what the company that made the building is going to do.
c)  ☐ gives examples of other buildings with similar problems.
d)  ☐ explains how the building got its name.
e)  ☐ gives an opinion of modern architecture in general.
f)  ☐ talks about how the building has affected nearby businesses.

**D  You are the manager of a shop affected by the 'Walkie Scorchie'. Write a letter of complaint to the developers explaining what your particular issue is and demand that they take action. Write about 200 words.**

# London's car-frying skyscraper

[1] London's skyline has a new addition: the Walkie Scorchie. Joining the crowded group of glass skyscrapers with nicknames such as the Shard, the Gherkin and the Cheese Grater, is 20 Fenchurch Street, which had previously been known as the Walkie Talkie, because it looked a little like a gigantic two-way radio. But the 37-storey office building has gained some new nicknames: the Death Ray, the Fryscraper, the Walkie Scorchie. This is because the building's south-facing side concentrates and reflects the sun's **rays** into an intense beam of light. Along a 30-metre stretch of pavement – not very far from where the Great Fire of 1666 started – London's burning.

[2] On Tuesday afternoon, I was sent out to see if I could fry an egg in the heat, a task that I thought was impossible on an  **overcast** September day. But, not only was it possible, I had to run out of the death ray that was slowly cooking my egg, because the thinning hairs on my head started to catch fire. On Monday, the air temperature in the concentrated beam reached 69.8° C (158° F). To put that in **context,** the world's hottest temperature was recorded in Death Valley, California, at 56.7° C (134° F) over 100 years ago. Dr Simon Foster, a physicist, accidentally left his measuring equipment in a black bag on the pavement for 10 minutes on Tuesday. The thermometer read 92.6° C (198.7° F). 'It's insane. It's just ridiculous. I've never felt heat like it,' he says.

[3] But while the Walkie Scorchie is causing much amusement to curious pedestrians coming to **gawk,** it is causing serious problems for the row of shops caught in its **glare.** Ali Akay of Re-Style barbers, opposite the tower, told me he was 'too stressed' to talk, but confirmed his carpet was burned on Tuesday and many of the plastic bottles of shampoo and hair gel in the window had started to melt. Diana Pham, assistant manager of the next-door Viet Café, admitted she was enjoying the extra business from office workers coming to get a little sunshine at lunchtime. But four tiles on the outside of her café have popped off the building in the last two days, and her furniture is starting to cook. 'The chairs started to smell very, very bad, like they were burning. We thought something terrible was happening,' she says. At the end of last week, the side mirror and panels of a businessman's car had all melted, after being parked outside the café for just two hours. Parking has now been **suspended** on the street.

[4] The developers responsible for 20 Fenchurch Street say that the building's glass has been there for months but only led to problems in the last few days, 'caused by the current location of the sun in the sky'. They promise they are working on a solution, which for now is likely to be a temporary **awning** to protect the shops.

[5] Architectural experts are not impressed and point out that too many modern skyscrapers are causing similar problems. Three years ago, residents at the Vdara hotel in Las Vegas – designed by the same architect as the Walkie Talkie – complained of being 'scorched' by the rays hitting the swimming pool area. The rays were melting their plastic drinking cups, guests claimed. In Dallas, the Museum Tower, a 42-storey apartment building, reflected so much light into the neighbouring Nasher Sculpture Center that it threatened artworks in the gallery, **scorched** plants and caused a two-year **dispute** between the two parties.

[6] For most of the Londoners in the area, however, the issue is not so much the heat being created, but the fact that a city full of masterpieces of traditional architecture is fast becoming a city of glass. As little as a decade ago, you could turn a corner and find a beautiful old **spire** amid the modern office towers. Now, your only guarantee is being blinded by the light.

Source: www.telegraph.co.uk

## 1 VOCABULARY: social issues

**A** 🎧 **19** Listen and write the words you hear.

1 _____   3 _____   5 _____   7 _____
2 _____   4 _____   6 _____   8 _____

**B** Complete the sentences with words from Exercise A.

1 Samira is a _____ – she had to leave her home country because of the war there.
2 There is a lot of _____ in this area because the unemployment rate is high
  and people don't have enough money to live on.
3 The group campaigns against _____ in the workplace and demands equality for all.
4 She's not only a successful singer, she's also an _____ for a children's charity.
5 All donations will go directly to _____ children to help give them a better start in life.
6 Xavier used his fortune to found a _____ organisation, which helps
  unemployed young people to find work.
7 Sergio received funding for his PhD from a scientific _____.
8 Aid workers have warned that the famine could become a _____ disaster.

## 2 GRAMMAR: *would rather* and *would prefer*

**A** Correct the mistakes in the sentences. Two sentences
are correct.

1 Sam would prefer not take part in the demonstration tomorrow.
2 Theo would rather get involved in student politics.
3 They would prefer donations not to be send by mail.
4 He would rather people volunteered in the hospital shop.
5 We would rather she not to volunteer anywhere dangerous.
6 We'd prefer not collect donations until tomorrow.

### WHAT'S RIGHT?

✗ I'd rather to donate time than money.

✓ _____
  _____

**B** Complete the text with the verbs from the box in the correct form.

give   go   invest   not/receive   not/transport   see

## EARTHQUAKE APPEAL

**We're very grateful for the overwhelming response from the public to our earthquake appeal.** We have plenty of tinned food items now, so we would prefer (1) _____ any more. Instead we would rather people (2) _____ warm clothes or bedding. In addition, local hospitals have reported that their blood supplies are running low. If you are able to donate blood, doctors would rather you (3) _____ directly to Central Hospital because they would prefer (4) _____ the blood from regional clinics. We are also asking for donations of money to help with rebuilding the area. We would rather (5) _____ in projects that will benefit the local community far into the future, so we will be consulting with local people to find out where they would prefer (6) _____ the money spent.

# 3 LISTENING: for main ideas

**A** You are going to listen to a business studies lecture. Number these topics in the order you think the speaker will talk about them.

a) ☐ the company's recent history

b) ☐ the story of the company's beginning

c) ☐ an overview of what the company does

**B** 🎧 **20** Listen to the lecture and check your answers.

**C** Listen again. Choose the sentence that best expresses the main idea of each part.

Main idea 1:
a) The company sells jewellery, items for the home, toys, games, baskets, stationery and many other things.
b) The company buys direct from producers at a fair price and sells through a number of different channels.
c) The company sells direct to customers at festivals.

Main idea 2:
a) Edna Ruth Byler was strongly affected by the situation of artisans in Puerto Rico in 1946 so she started a company to help them.
b) The name of Edna Ruth Byler's first company was the Overseas Needlepoint and Crafts Project.
c) Edna Ruth Byler is no longer involved in running the company.

Main idea 3:
a) The company turned 50 in 1996.
b) Ten Thousand Villages won an important award.
c) After 50 years in business, the company changed its name and expanded.

**D** Choose the correct options to complete the sentences.

1 Ten Thousand Villages makes / doesn't make a profit.
2 The artisans make handcrafted items and sell / donate them to Ten Thousand Villages.
3 Ten Thousand Villages sells the products in over 17 / 70 shops throughout the USA.
4 Edna Ruth Byler came from the USA / Puerto Rico.
5 She started an organisation called Ten Thousand Villages / Overseas Needlepoint and Crafts Project.
6 She bought products from artisans and sold them in North America / developing countries.
7 In 1996, the company was 30 / 50 years old.
8 The company started selling online in 1997 / 2006.

## 4 VOCABULARY: social justice

**A  Match the sentences (1–6) with their same meanings (a–f).**

1   Some governments provide benefits for people living in poverty.
2   Some countries can't afford to help their own citizens.
3   Governments have a responsibility to help people get work.
4   If you're poor, you have the right to government benefits.
5   Almost every country has citizens who don't have enough to live on.
6   Almost every country has unemployed people.

a)   Leaders of countries have an obligation to help people find employment.
b)   Poor people are entitled to receive money from the government.
c)   There are people who are out of work all over the world.
d)   In some countries, money for the poor is available from the government.
e)   Everywhere there are people who can't manage to survive with what they have.
f)   Some governments don't have enough money to give to people who need it.

**B  Complete the ad with the correct form of the words and phrases from the box.**

| benefits    can afford to    have a responsibility to |
| have the right to    live on    unemployed |

Everyone (1) _____ food, clothing and shelter. But 842 million people in the world do not have enough to eat. Many of them go hungry because they (2) _____ buy enough food. Others don't have enough to eat because there simply isn't enough food available. Many of the world's hungry are (3) _____, and have no access to government (4) _____. If you have enough to eat, then you (5) _____ help those who do not. A donation of just a few pounds a day is enough for someone in need to (6) _____.

Please give generously to Give Food Now.

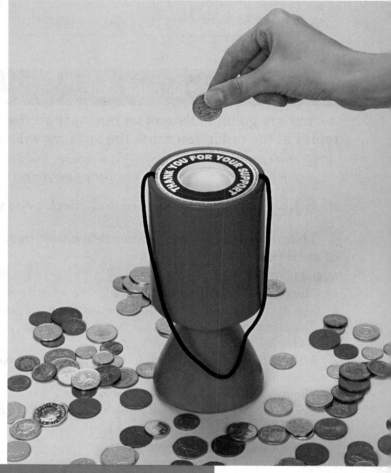

## 5 GRAMMAR: noun clauses as subjects

**A  Write the letter of the correct form for each sentence.**

a)   Question word is the subject        b)   Question word is the object

1   ___ What the government needs to do is provide better benefits.
2   ___ What's difficult to understand is the scale of the poverty.
3   ___ Who gains the most from this funding is debatable.
4   ___ How people donate money is not important.
5   ___ Where you decide to volunteer can make a big difference.
6   ___ What happens next is up to the local people.

**WHAT'S RIGHT?**

(X) What does the charity need is …

(✓) _____
_____

**B** Put the words in the correct order to make sentences.

1 themselves / feed / to / what / need / people / way / a / is

_____

2 the / who / receives / aid / uncertain / most / is

_____

3 donations / year / where / send / this / undecided / we / is

_____

4 we / distribute / is / food / what / do / of / baskets

_____

5 community / important / our / how / is / we / support

_____

6 donate / what's / to / direct / best / is / money

_____

## 6 WRITING: sentence variety

**A** Match each sentence (1–7) with a grammatical structure (a–g).

1 Seeing that news story made me sad.
2 Everyone has a responsibility to help others.
3 I want to get people to take the issue seriously.
4 If we work together, we can make a difference.
5 It's helpful to give even a small amount.
6 What I'd like to do is make it easier for people to give.
7 The donations, which I collect, are given to charity.

a) regular subject + verb + object

b) noun clause as subject

c) gerund as subject

d) *it's* + adjective + infinitive

e) conditional

f) relative clause

g) causative (*have/get sth. done* or *have sb. do/get sb. to do sth.*)

**B** Rewrite sentences 1–6 from the paragraph, using the grammatical structures and prompts below.

# Helping the homeless
## *close to home*

(1) It may surprise you to discover how many homeless people there are in your area. (2) They really need your support to help them get back on their feet. (3) But knowing how to get involved in charity work is not always easy. (4) You could make a significant contribution by volunteering in some way. (5) Charities may be the main source of funding for local homeless shelters and often need volunteers. Or you could turn your hand to fundraising: (6) you could think of new and exciting ways of persuading people to donate money to the charity.

1 **gerund as subject:** Discovering _____

2 **noun clause as subject:** What they really need _____

3 ***it's* + adjective + infinitive:** But it's not always easy _____

4 **conditional:** If you volunteer _____

5 **relative clause:** Charities, _____, may be the main source of funding for local homeless shelters.

6 **causative:** You could think of new and exciting ways of _____

# SkillsStudio

**A** Read the article and answer the question below.

## Ben Affleck at the Senate in Washington

Actor and director Ben Affleck left Hollywood behind this week when he appeared at the Senate to talk to the Committee on Foreign Relations about violence in the Democratic Republic of Congo. Other celebrity humanitarians with good intentions have visited the Senate in the past but have been unpersuasive when questioned by senators.

Affleck, however, was knowledgeable about the subject and spoke well about the complex situation in the region. He outlined ways that the US government could help, including increasing agricultural aid and guaranteeing fair elections. Affleck proved his commitment to the region in 2010 by setting up the Eastern Congo Initiative, a US-based organisation, which provides support and grants for people in eastern Congo. Affleck says that, apart from his family and his work, this is what he wants to be remembered for, so he takes it very seriously.

**According to the article, why did Ben Affleck speak to the Senate Committee on Foreign Relations?**

a) Because he wanted to show the US government how it can help deal with violence in the Democratic Republic of Congo.

b) Because he wanted his Eastern Congo Initiative to be taken seriously.

c) Because he wanted to get the US government to provide grants for his Eastern Congo Initiative.

**B** 🎧 **21** Listen to a radio debate and answer these questions.

1 Which speaker thinks that celebrities' humanitarian efforts can do more good than harm?

_____

2 Which speaker thinks that celebrities' humanitarian efforts can do more harm than good?

_____

**C** Listen again and choose the correct answer.

1 Paul Cunard is a …
   a) radio host.
   b) journalist.
   c) representative of the Kitts Humanitarian Foundation.

2 Paul thinks that celebrities do charity work to …
   a) raise the profile of the charity.
   b) help poor people.
   c) make money for themselves.

3 Nahla argues that we shouldn't generalise about …
   a) celebrities' intentions.
   b) celebrities' profiles.
   c) the issues that celebrities care about.

4 Nahla thinks that celebrities may feel …
  a) a less strong sense of responsibility to help others than non-celebrities.
  b) a stronger sense of responsibility to help others than non-celebrities.
  c) just as strong a sense of responsibility to help others as non-celebrities.

5 Paul thinks that Live 8 was …
  a) about making money rather than tackling global poverty.
  b) controlled by the corporate sponsors.
  c) about getting governments to promise to deal with poverty.

6 Paul says that the sales of some of the Live 8 artists went up by … after the concert.
  a) 36,000%     b) 3600%     c) 360%

7 Paul thinks that the presence of celebrities leads people to focus on … of problems.
  a) short-term symptoms and causes
  b) short-term causes rather than long-term symptoms
  c) short term symptoms rather than long-term causes

8 Nahla mentions Ben Affleck's Eastern Congo Initiative as an example of a celebrity who …
  a) has raised awareness of a short-term crisis.
  b) is committed to addressing the long-term issues in a country.
  c) has used his charity to raise his profile.

**D Listen again and match the words you heard in the debate (1–8) with their correct meanings (a–h).**

1 representative (n.)
2 profile (n.)
3 outweigh (v.)
4 highlight (v.)
5 found (v.)
6 naïve (adj.)
7 corporate (adj.)
8 sustainable (adj.)

a) public image
b) draw attention to
c) innocent, showing lack of experience
d) establish, set up
e) a group of people acting together, for example, in business
f) a person acting on behalf of someone or something
g) be more important than
h) capable of being continued

**E Listen again and complete the phrases you hear.**

1 Would you like to _____ in here?
2 I _____ what you're saying.
3 Would you like to _____ to that?
4 I couldn't _____ more.
5 I see your _____ .
6 We're just going to have to _____ to disagree on this.

**F Write the numbers of the phrases from Exercise E next to their function.**

a) ☐☐ To invite somebody to contribute to a conversation
b) ☐☐ To admit that something somebody else has said is true
c) ☐☐ To show that you don't agree with something

**G Write an email of about 250 words to the radio station in response to the programme, giving your opinion on the debate.**

# UNIT 9 COMPETITIVE EDGE

## 1 GRAMMAR: gerunds after prepositions

**A  Choose the correct options to complete the sentences.**

1  People who worry about / of losing generally do not look forward for / to competing with others.
2  However, those who feel they are good at / on doing something are often excited with / about demonstrating their abilities in competitions.
3  If you are bored for / by exercising alone, you might enjoy a competitive sport like football or tennis.
4  It's not healthy for children to care about / on winning too much; they should only be interested in / of having fun and doing their best.
5  It's natural not to be happy to / about losing a match, but too many athletes today complain about / for losing because of decisions made by the referee.

**B  Complete the text with the correct form of the verb or adjective from the box.**

> bored   capable   excited   happy   insist   interested   look   object   responsible

**Mark Lewis**
Check this out! I'm really (1) _____ forward to seeing this in October. Anyone else?

**Jenny Vega**
Yeah, I'm very (2) _____ in seeing this. Mark, you still have six months before the competition. Maybe you can grow a beard and enter the contest?

**Mark Lewis**
Ha ha! I'm not (3) _____ of growing a long beard in such a short time. Also, I think my girlfriend Lisa might (4) _____ to seeing it every day.

**Lisa Green**
Mark, if you (5) _____ on growing a beard, I won't mind. It's true that I'm not a fan of beards and I wouldn't be (6) _____ about looking at it every day, but I think that after a few weeks you'd be (7) _____ with having it.

**Mark Lewis**
Lisa, really? OK, then I'm going to grow one. Wow, I'm pretty (8) _____ about doing this!

**Jenny Vega**
Uh-oh. Sorry, Lisa, I guess I'm (9) _____ for starting this!

This year's World Beard and Moustache Championships will be held in Leogang, Austria. Will you be there?

👍 Like    Share

## WHAT'S RIGHT?

Ⓧ As a parent, I object to have beauty contests for children.

✓ _____
_____

Ⓧ Would you like to playing football in the park on Sunday?

✓ _____
_____

## 2 READING: understanding text organisation

**A  Read the text about the science of competition. What two things does it say about people who feel very worried in stressful situations?**

a)  Scientists are developing a chemical that will help them.
b)  They may have a gene that makes them worry.
c)  They always score lower on important exams.
d)  With the right attitude, they can perform very well.

# The Science of Competition

¹ From football matches to corporate boardrooms, what helps us win? In their new book, *Top Dog: The Science of Winning and Losing*, bestselling authors Po Bronson and Ashley Merryman investigate the science behind competition.

² Most of us feel anxious before stressful situations **(1)** such as exams, job interviews or sports competitions. Knowing the importance of the moment, our heart rate increases, our palms sweat and our knees go weak. However, there are also people who simply don't feel stressed. Why? Genetics, say the experts. In stressful situations, the body produces a brain chemical called dopamine. Some people have methionine, **(2)** a special kind of gene that makes the brain reabsorb dopamine more slowly. In a stressful situation, **(3)** people who have the gene have a flood of dopamine in the brain, creating the sensation of worry.

³ 'The nickname for people with this gene is the worriers,' Merryman explains. 'In periods of stress … they have that flood of dopamine to the brain, and the brain just sort of shuts down.'

⁴ If you're a worrier, don't lose hope. Merryman says that your brain can adjust to routine stress – **(4)** in other words, you can thrive in high-pressure situations as long as they're familiar to you.

⁵ A small change in attitude can also help worriers succeed. In a recent study, scientists focused on two groups of Harvard students taking the GREs, the American graduate school entrance exam. Before the test, researchers told one group of students that anxiety could actually improve their performance. Those students scored 50 points higher on a practice exam, and 65 points higher on the actual test.

⁶ So if you're someone who doesn't perform well in stressful situations, just remember this experiment. You can work on processing information in ways that increase your chances of success.

**Adapted from WGBH's "Innovation Hub"**

**B** Look at the underlined phrases in the article. Write the number of the phrase that answers the questions.

a) ☐ What is methionine and what does it do?
b) ☐ How does dopamine affect some people in stressful situations?
c) ☐ According to the article, what are some examples of stressful situations?
d) ☐ How can the brain adjust to stress?

**C** Look at the underlined phrases in the article. Which phrase or phrases …

a) ☐ define a word or say what something is?
b) ☐ explain how something happens?
c) ☐ give examples of something?

## 3 VOCABULARY: expressions of emotion

Complete the comments on the article in Section 2 with the words from the box.

| a desire to | a feeling of | the agony of | the fun of | the will to |

**Tom H:** I definitely have the worrier gene. As a child, I always had **(1)** _____ anxiety and dread before my football matches, and now, before a big presentation, I always feel **(2)** _____ run away!

**Marisol:** Life is too short to worry! Instead of worrying about feeling **(3)** _____ defeat if you lose, just try to enjoy **(4)** _____ playing and competing!

**Erica:** I'm not a worrier, but I hate contests and competitions. I guess I just don't have **(5)** _____ win.

## 4 GRAMMAR: verb + gerund

### A Find and correct five mistakes.

Every evening, millions of families around the world sit at home watch reality TV. We know we shouldn't waste time to watch these programmes, but we have a good time laugh at them. They're harmless fun. Or are they? According to a recent survey of girls aged 11–17, those who like to watch reality TV are more competitive than those who don't. They are more likely to agree with statements such as, 'You have to lie to get what you want', 'I have a hard time to trust other girls' and 'It's normal for girls to gossip and compete with each other'. However, the effects of reality TV were not all negative. Sixty-two per cent of the girls who watched reality TV said they found themselves to learn about new things and important issues.

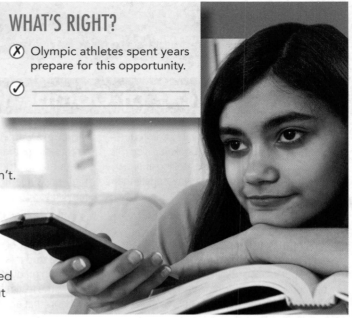

### WHAT'S RIGHT?

(✗) Olympic athletes spent years prepare for this opportunity.

(✓) _____

### B Complete the paragraphs with the correct form of the words from the box.

find   have trouble   listen   perform   sit   solve   spend   think

If you **(1)** _____ relaxing during high-pressure events, you may benefit from positive visualisation. The technique is simple. In the days before the event, close your eyes for a few minutes and imagine **(2)** _____ successfully. You can do it anywhere, but it is best to lie down in a comfortable place **(3)** _____ to gentle music. If you **(4)** _____ a few minutes a day visualising, you will probably feel calmer and more confident on the day of the event.

For many, it's a favourite Sunday ritual to **(5)** _____ at the kitchen table doing the crossword puzzle. You can **(6)** _____ people working on crosswords everywhere – even on the Underground. If you love crosswords and have no difficulty **(7)** _____ the most challenging ones, you may want to enter the annual UK Times National Crossword Championship, where, the world's fastest 'solvers' compete for a £1,000 prize. Because they can't waste time **(8)** _____ of the answers, competitors often prepare by memorising clues and answers from old puzzles.

## 5 VOCABULARY: scientific nouns and verbs

Choose the correct options to complete the text.

### Is it *healthy* to be *competitive?*

**Competitive or easygoing – which type are you? Why does it matter?** **(1)** Research / Theory in the 1950s (and through the 1970s) seemed to **(2)** measure / prove that competitive Type A personalities had a higher risk of heart attacks and heart disease than Type Bs. This supported the common stereotype of the competitive business executive who rushes around, working late hours, until he finally has a heart attack. (The early **(3)** theories / studies were all done on men, by the way).

After **(4)** researching / proving the issue more, however, many experts now doubt the original **(5)** conclusions / measurements. They now think that only some parts of the Type A personality are connected with heart attacks: hostility, aggression and difficulty expressing positive emotions.

This has led scientists to develop a new **(6)** theory / measurement. Perhaps the aggressive Type As have a higher risk of heart disease because they try to do everything themselves and become too stressed? They are not good team players and rarely let others help them. They also have trouble reducing stress because they are not good at expressing their emotions.

In future **(7)** experiments / conclusions, researchers may want to examine the hearts of Type A people more closely. This will help them **(8)** experiment / measure their risk of heart attacks more accurately. For now, if you are a Type A personality, it is probably a good idea to be **(9)** tested / experimented for heart problems.

**A  Read this text and choose the best paraphrases for the underlined sentences.**

1  a)  Many people think that winning or losing in 'Rock, Paper, Scissors' is mostly about luck.

   b)  Everyone thinks that winning in the game is all about luck.

2  a)  The most frequent opening gesture is 'rock', according to statistics.

   b)  Statistics show that players with less experience usually begin a game by playing the 'rock' gesture.

3  a)  You should play scissors first to beat experienced players because they'll know the tactic and will begin with paper.

   b)  If you are playing an experienced opponent who already knows this strategy, begin by playing scissors because your experienced opponent will begin with paper.

4  a)  The other player will probably make a different gesture the third time because they think this will be more difficult to predict.

   b)  So that you can't guess what play they will make, your opponent won't make the same gesture three times in a row.

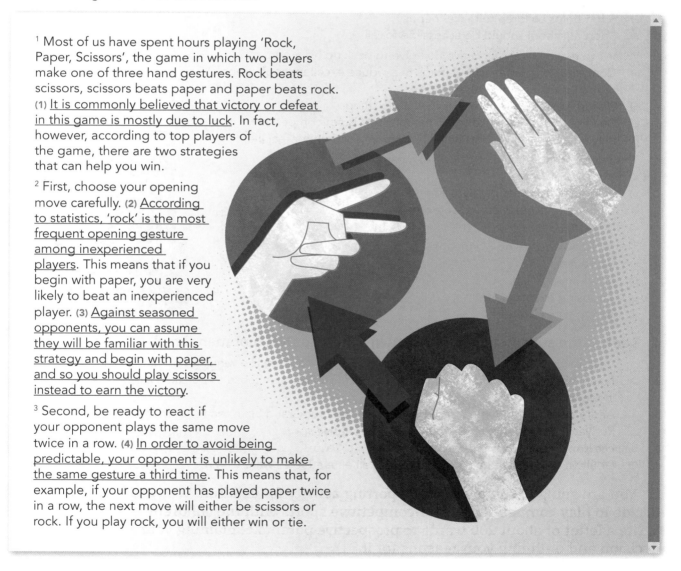

¹ Most of us have spent hours playing 'Rock, Paper, Scissors', the game in which two players make one of three hand gestures. Rock beats scissors, scissors beats paper and paper beats rock. **(1) It is commonly believed that victory or defeat in this game is mostly due to luck.** In fact, however, according to top players of the game, there are two strategies that can help you win.

² First, choose your opening move carefully. **(2) According to statistics, 'rock' is the most frequent opening gesture among inexperienced players.** This means that if you begin with paper, you are very likely to beat an inexperienced player. **(3) Against seasoned opponents, you can assume they will be familiar with this strategy and begin with paper, and so you should play scissors instead to earn the victory.**

³ Second, be ready to react if your opponent plays the same move twice in a row. **(4) In order to avoid being predictable, your opponent is unlikely to make the same gesture a third time.** This means that, for example, if your opponent has played paper twice in a row, the next move will either be scissors or rock. If you play rock, you will either win or tie.

**B  🎧 22 Listen to two friends discuss the story and check your answers to Exercise A.**

# SkillsStudio

**A  Read the opinion article from a news site. Choose the correct options.**

1   According to a recent survey, most children think that sport should / should not be competitive.

2   Les Roopanarine believes that children's sport should / should not be competitive.

3   Dr Steve Bull believes that children's sport should / should not be competitive.

**B  Read the article again. Choose the correct answers.**

1   Les Roopanarine believes that children enjoy sports …
   a)   if they start playing at a young age, like Rafael Nadal.
   b)   if they play with friends.
   c)   if they are not under pressure to win.
   d)   if they work hard to improve their skills and technique.

2   On which point do the two contributors agree?
   a)   Sport teaches children how to work as a part of a team.
   b)   Sport helps children to stay healthy.
   c)   Sport helps children to make friends.
   d)   Sport at school should be accessible for all.

3   What two reasons does Dr Steve Bull give to back up his argument?
   a)   Competitive sport at school helps to produce excellent sportspeople of the future.
   b)   Children like competition because it's exciting.
   c)   Children don't bother to try so hard if sport is not competitive.
   d)   Playing competitive sport helps to prepare children for real life.

4   The word *essence* (line 4 and line 38) means …
   a)   excitement.
   b)   the most important part of something.
   c)   the least important part of something.
   d)   popularity.

5   The word *adversity* (line 74) means …
   a)   bad times in life.
   b)   good times in life.
   c)   surprising events in life.
   d)   boring times in life.

**C  Look at the statements. Write T (true), F (false) or NM (not mentioned).**

1   ___ According to a recent survey, 64% of children said that they like winning and hate losing.

2   ___ Rafael Nadal could have been a professional footballer, but chose to pursue a career in tennis instead.

3   ___ Andre Agassi was the first male player to win all four Grand Slam tennis tournaments.

4   ___ Rudyard Kipling used to enjoy playing competitive sport.

5   ___ Les Roopanarine used to be a teacher.

6   ___ Dr Steve Bull says that, in his experience, all elite athletes want to win.

**D  You are going to run a weekend sporting activity for children. Will you decide to play competitive or non-competitive sports with the children? Write a letter of about 200 words to prospective parents explaining your decision and outlining your reasons for it.**

# Does it matter if children don't care *about winning?*

Most schoolchildren would be 'relieved or not bothered' if games were no longer competitive, a survey has found. But would sport lose its essence? Our contributors debate the issue.

**Les Roopanarine, sports journalist and author**
A bright future beckons for British sport, judging by the findings of a survey commissioned by the Marylebone Cricket Club and the Chance to Shine charity. The study suggests that 64% of the nation's schoolchildren just don't care whether they win or lose. Good for them. Unburdened by fear of failure, they will be free to enjoy the simple pleasures of kicking, throwing or batting a ball, running at full pelt, or simply jumping as high or as far as they can. That in turn will afford them space to grow and learn without any weight of expectation; to make friends and acquire fresh skills, hone technique and hopefully lay down lasting roots with their favourite pursuits.

No one is denying that you need to start early to be successful. Yet there are more professional athletes like Rafael Nadal – whose enjoyment of different sports was such that he had to choose between tennis and football at the age of 12 – than Andre Agassi, who, pressured by his father throughout his childhood, prospered as a tennis player despite coming to hate the game.

Commentators who believe that the indifference of British kids towards winning or losing means we're in danger of not producing great sportspeople in the next generation are wrong. Enjoyment and achievement are not mutually exclusive. Besides, didn't Rudyard Kipling promise us the earth if we could meet with triumph and disaster and treat them just the same?

**Dr Steve Bull, performance psychologist and author**
Kipling was right – absolutely. However, by its very definition, the term 'sport' involves (indeed requires) competition. That's what sport is – physical activity in which people compete against each other. If you remove the competitive element you lose the essence. The problem we have here is that many young people, for a whole host of different reasons, have not been allowed to learn and develop within an environment in which sport is encouraged. I began my career as a PE teacher in the early 1980s when competitive sport was still thriving. I taught in a school which sometimes fielded three rugby teams in the under-12 age group. I can still recall the excitement that those pupils experienced on a Saturday morning. They were playing to win and loving the competition. We need to help our youngsters connect with the essential joy of running around with your mates trying to win 'together'.

**Les Roopanarine**
There's no doubting the importance of teamwork. But I also think there's a big difference between running around with your mates for fun and doing so in the pursuit of victory. It seems ironic that, while elite sportspeople are often encouraged by psychologists to forget about winning and losing and instead focus on process, we believe our children should do the opposite. If two-thirds of schoolchildren say they would be 'relieved or not bothered' if games were no longer competitive, then we should listen. Because younger kids don't think like adults; where we might regard winning and losing as the end of the world, to them dwelling on medals or misfortunes comes a distant second to enjoyment.

**Dr Steve Bull**
An interesting response but sport psychologists generally do not encourage athletes to 'forget' about winning – it's more that the most effective way of achieving success is to focus on the 'process' during the actual performance. In 30 years of being a sport psychologist I have yet to come across an elite performer who doesn't care about winning. It's a cliché, I know, but life is not fair. Competitive sport is a great way of preparing young people for the 'real world' in which things will not always go their way. Learning how to deal with adversity, bounce back from disappointment and accept that luck isn't always on your side are important lessons for children to absorb before they step out in to the world of work.

*Adapted from http://www.theguardian.com/commentisfree/2014/apr/26/does-matter-children-care-about-winning-games-sport*

# UNIT 10 RISKY BUSINESS

## 1 VOCABULARY: safety and risk

**A** ))) 23 **Listen and write the words or phrases you hear.**

1 _____  5 _____
2 _____  6 _____
3 _____  7 _____
4 _____  8 _____

**B** **Complete the sentences with the correct form of words or phrases from Exercise A.**

1 Theo would like to have the _____ of working for himself, but he needs the _____ of a steady job right now.

2 Starting my own business was _____, but I _____ and now it's really successful.

3 I think that if you _____ risk at an early age, then you're less likely to _____ when you grow up.

4 Jan _____ take on the new challenge and didn't let her fear of _____ stop her.

## 2 GRAMMAR: expressing ability

**A** **What form goes after these verbs? Write I (infinitive), B (base form) or G (gerund) for each verb.**

1 be good at ___
2 (not) succeed in ___
3 (not) manage ___
4 can/can't ___
5 be incapable of ___
6 could/couldn't ___
7 be unable ___
8 be able ___
9 be capable of ___

**B** **Choose the correct options (a, b or c) to complete the text.**

**Wing walking – not an easy sport at all**
Posted by Pete209   5th May   2 Comments   [SHARE]   [SUGGESTIONS]

Expert wing walkers manage **(1)** _____ death-defying stunts for millions of spectators below. How do they do it? Well, they have to be good at **(2)** _____ their nerves, be capable of **(3)** _____ on a wing while doing stunts, be able **(4)** _____ their emotions and succeed in **(5)** _____ their balance in strong winds. Oh, and they have to be able **(6)** _____ heights. It's pretty easy, really. Do you think you could **(7)** _____ it? ☺

1 a) to perform     b) perform     c) performing
2 a) to overcome    b) overcome    c) overcoming
3 a) to balance     b) balance     c) balancing
4 a) to control     b) control     c) controlling
5 a) to keep        b) keep        c) keeping
6 a) to cope with   b) cope with   c) coping with
7 a) to do          b) do          c) doing

### WHAT'S RIGHT?

✗ You have to be capable of take risks to run your own business.

✓ _____

## 3 WRITING: requesting action

**A** **Read the letter. Choose the function of each paragraph.**

1  a) describe a problem      b) make suggestions      c) complain about the site
2  a) make suggestions       b) state requests         c) express confidence
3  a) thank the recipient     b) explain a problem      c) show trust in the recipient

Dear Mr Fielder,

**(1)** We are writing to draw your attention to a problem we noticed at the adventure playground recently constructed at Oldham Park. The teenagers who use the tower there often muck around and push each other off the platform. We are concerned that they could easily injure themselves or each other.

**(2)** With this in mind, we would like you to consider making the following changes to the adventure playground:

- Place rubber on the laminated wood to prevent slipping.
- Place a rubber safety surface on the ground below the platform to prevent injury to anyone who may fall while playing.

**(3)** We would like to mention that we are happy with the adventure playground. Since it was built, our teenagers have spent a lot of time outdoors. However, we feel that the suggestions above would reduce the risk of injury. Thank you in advance for your assistance. We are confident that you will take prompt action regarding this matter.

Yours sincerely,

*Peter Barker*

on behalf of The Oldham Park Residents' Committee

**B** **Find expressions in the letter in Exercise A that have the same meaning as the sentences below. Write them next to the sentence.**

a) We want you to think about … _____
b) We want to tell you about something we are aware of … _____
c) We know you'll do something about it quickly. _____
d) We want to say that we like … _____

**C** **Number the paragraphs in the letter in the correct order. Then complete the letter with the answers from Exercise B.**

Dear Mrs Carter,

☐ **(1)** _____ the decision to install a lift in the shopping centre because it is very useful for elderly people like myself and saves us having to climb the stairs! **(2)** _____

☐ **(3)** _____ taking the following action:

- Close off the lift so that children can't play in it.
- Fix the lift as soon as possible.

☐ **(4)** _____ in the new shopping centre — the lift is broken and children were playing in it, which is dangerous.

Yours sincerely,

Jody Hills

## 4 VOCABULARY: expressions with *risk*

**A** Match the words and phrases (1–6) to their definitions (a–f).

| | | | |
|---|---|---|---|
| 1 | risk your life | a) | a study of the dangers or hazards |
| 2 | risky | b) | in danger |
| 3 | at risk | c) | do something that involves danger |
| 4 | risk assessment | d) | dangerous, hazardous |
| 5 | run the risk | e) | make the dangers smaller in size or number |
| 6 | reduce the risks | f) | do something that is so dangerous you might die |

**B** Complete the blog with the words and expressions from Exercise A in the correct form.

HOME   FOOTBALL   RUGBY   TENNIS   GOLF   MOTOR RACING   CYCLING   CRICKET        OTHER SPORTS

## *All Sports Blog*

NEWS

FEATURES

OPINION

VIDEOS

BLOG

PODCAST

Pages (3) 1 2 3 4 5

### BASE jumping: too dangerous?

Marie101
873 posts

23/10 08.44

People (1) _____ every day to do dangerous sports. I mean, BASE jumping off buildings is so (2) _____ that it's illegal in most countries. There would be no point in carrying out a (3) _____ of this sport because it would be off the scale! Maybe if more BASE jumpers wore helmets, it would (4) _____ of injury?

JJracer
moderator

23/10 08.58

I doubt it. People would still (5) _____ of dying even if more of them wore helmets. They're selfish people. They put other people's lives (6) _____ because if they get into trouble, then somebody has to come out and rescue them.

## 5 GRAMMAR: past modals of deduction

**A** What is the function of these modal verbs? Write *SP* (strong probability), *MP* (moderate probability/improbability) or *SI* (strong improbability) for each modal verb.

| | | | | | |
|---|---|---|---|---|---|
| 1 | couldn't have: _____ | 4 | may (not) have: _____ | 6 | must not have: _____ |
| 2 | might (not) have: _____ | 5 | can't have: _____ | 7 | could have: _____ |
| 3 | must have: _____ | | | | |

**B  Choose the correct options to complete the text.**

How did the magician Harry Houdini manage to escape from handcuffs?
In the 1920s, no one had seen escape artists like Houdini before. It
(1) may have / must have looked like magic. Of course, now we know that
he (2) couldn't have / might have used special powers. So how did he do it?
We don't know. Some people think that he (3) may have / may not have
been helped by someone, which is possible. Many modern magicians hide
a key between their teeth. Houdini (4) might not have / could have done
that too. A few people think that he (5) couldn't have / might have opened
the lock from memory, but that seems unlikely. Whatever his secret, it
(6) must have / may have been an incredible sight!

**WHAT'S RIGHT?**

Ⓧ He couldn't think it was
risky, or he wouldn't have
done it.

Ⓥ _____
_____
_____

**C  Complete the conversation with the correct form of the verbs in brackets.**

**Al:**  Wow, you ran a risk there! Riding that elephant (1) _____
(can't/be) very safe. You (2) _____ (might/fall off).

**Maya:**  Well, you risked your life when you went on that camel! It (3) _____
(might/throw) you off! You (4) _____ (could/have) a terrible accident.

**Sue:**  Well, I think you're both crazy. It (5) _____ (may not/seem) risky at
the time, but you (6) _____ (could/be) seriously injured.

## 6 LISTENING: rapid speech

**A  »🎧24  Listen to the conversation and complete the sentence.**

The two friends are discussing …
1  the care that the boy with the broken arm received after his accident.
2  whether children should take risks when they play.
3  how parents should always take responsibility for their children's injuries.

**B  Listen to the conversation again and choose T (true)
or F (false).**

1  The recreation area of the park has been closed off.
   T / F
2  The boy broke his arm when the slide collapsed on top of him.
   T / F
3  Mae thinks that children learn important skills by taking risks.
   T / F
4  Jenny doesn't have children.
   T / F

**C  Listen to the conversation again. Complete the
phrases you hear.**

1  _____ you hear that they've closed off …?
2  … they _____ decided that it's unsafe.
3  You've _____ be kidding.
4  It's _____ extreme.
5  I think parents just _____ keep …
6  I _____ about that.
7  That kid _____ fallen out of bed …
8  You've _____ point.

# SkillsStudio

**A** 🎧 **25** **Guess the answers to these questions. Then listen to a talk by Joe Scott and check your answers.**

1 Mount Kanchengjunga is the second / third highest mountain in the world.
2 It's on the border of India and Nepal / Pakistan.
3 It was first climbed in 1855 / 1955 by a team of British climbers.

**B** **Choose the best summary of Joe's talk.**

Joe's talk is about …
a) climbing Mount Kanchengjunga and what his next expedition will be.
b) his most recent expedition and his motivation for climbing mountains.
c) how dangerous it is to climb Mount Kanchengjunga.

**C** **Listen again and write the topics in the order you hear them talked about.**

☐ Joe's climb up Mount Kanchengjunga
☐ Facts and figures about Mount Kanchengjunga
☐ Joe's plans for the future
☐ The dangers associated with Mount Kanchengjunga
☐ The reasons why Joe loves climbing

**D** **Listen and match the words that you heard (1–6) with their correct definitions (a–f).**

1 a summit (*n.*)
2 sacred (*adj.*)
3 an avalanche (*n.*)
4 a thrill-seeker (*adj.*)
5 reckless (*adj.*)
6 rewarding (*adj.*)

a) a fall of snow down a mountain
b) without caring about danger
c) the highest point
d) providing personal satisfaction
e) someone who enjoys risky activities
f) holy or connected to religion

**E  Complete the sentences with a word or a short phrase.**

1   Joe starts by asking the audience to _____ if they know something about Mount Kanchengjunga.

2   Mount Kanchengjunga is _____ high and is the _____ highest mountain in the world.

3   Mount Everest and K2 are both _____ than Mount Kanchengjunga but Joe thinks that Mount Everest is _____ to climb than Mount Kanchengjunga.

4   Joe went up the _____ face of the mountain.

5   Joe thinks that the most dangerous things for climbers of Kanchengjunga are _____.

6   _____ of the mountaineers who have tried to climb Kanchengjunga have died in the attempt.

7   Joe _____ that extreme sportspeople must be risk-takers.

8   Joe describes his most recent climb as one of the most _____ of his life.

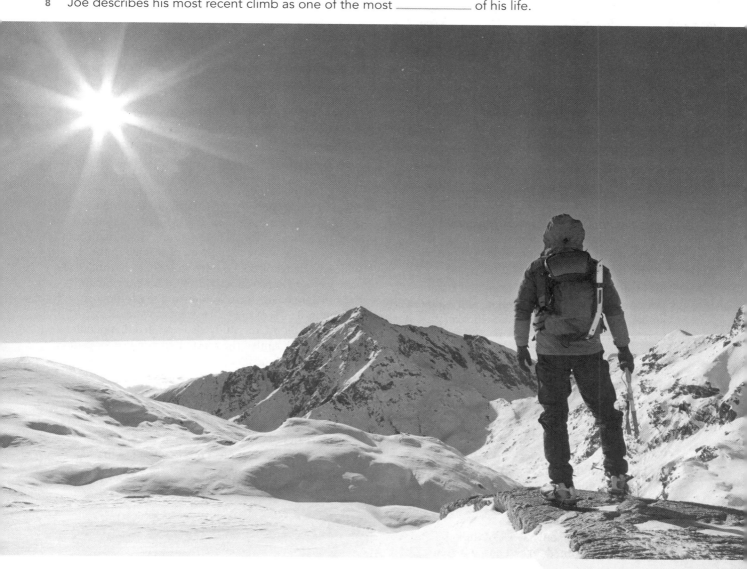

**F  Read the quote below. In your notebook write an opinion essay of about 300 words. Explain what you think Mark Zuckerberg means. Do you agree or disagree with this opinion?**

'The biggest risk is not taking any risk.' (Mark Zuckerberg)

## 1 READING: understanding text organisation

**A** Read and complete the text with sentences A–F below. There is one extra sentence that you do not need to use.

A This means that the researchers considered the artistic intentions of each individual image as well as analysing the overall trends and patterns that emerged according to location.

B This includes an essay about 'Imagined Data Communities' by Nadav Hachman, and a blog 'Gender, Age, and Ambiguity of Selfies on Instagram' by Mehrdrad Yazdani.

C So, overall, women clearly take significantly more selfies than men.

D This theory turned out to be true in the Selfiecity findings – Bangkok had the youngest subjects with an average age of 21.0 years and New York City was the oldest city with an average age of 25.3 years.

E One example of this is that women struck more extreme poses than men – the average amount of head tilt for women was 50% higher than for men (12.3° instead of 8.2°).

F Surprisingly though, only 3–5% of the photographs examined turned out to be selfies.

[1] Recent research has revealed some interesting trends in selfies taken in different parts of the world. Selfiecity is a project that was led by Dr Lev Manovich and Software Studies Initiative. It set out to investigate the style of selfies taken in five different cities: Bangkok, Berlin, Moscow, New York City and São Paulo. They randomly selected 120,000 photos (20,000–30,000 per city) from a total of 656,000 images collected on Instagram and analysed them to see if they were selfies. Given that everyone everywhere is talking about selfies right now, you might expect the percentage of selfies to be very high. **(1)** ____ The selfies that were selected for this research project were treated as a form of self-expression as well as a shared social experience. **(2)** ____
[2] The selfies were analysed in various ways including the age, gender, mood and poses of the subjects of the selfies. It is generally accepted that most selfies are taken by young people, particularly the under 30s. **(3)** ____ The average age of men was higher than that of women in every city. There was one trend that was true in all cities – the proportion of women in the selfies. In Bangkok 55.2% were women, in Berlin 59.4% were women, in New York City 61.6% were women, in São Paulo 65.4% were women and in Moscow an enormous 82.0% of the selfies were of women! **(4)** ____ In terms of mood, the study also revealed that people from Bangkok smiled the most often, while people in Moscow smiled the least.
[3] More in-depth analysis of Selfiecity's findings is available on their website. **(5)** ____ In addition, visitors to the site can navigate through some of the selfies either by searching the different cities or by examining specific characteristics of the subjects. Whatever the future holds for selfies, this project represents a fascinating snapshot of the kinds of selfies that are being taken around the world right now.

Source: http://selfiecity.net/#

**B** What are the functions of the sentences that were missing in Exercise A?

Which sentence …

1 summarises what comes before it? ____
2 presents a further explanation of an important idea? ____
3 provides evidence against a point of view mentioned? ____
4 provides evidence in support of a claim? ____
5 gives specific examples of something mentioned? ____

## 2 VOCABULARY: describing photographs

**Complete the texts with words or phrases from the box.**

| background | foreground | in focus | landscape | left-hand side | out of focus |
| portrait | right-hand side | subject |

This photograph is a beautiful **(1)** _____ of a lake in Banff National Park in Canada. It's easy to understand why the photographer chose this location as the **(2)** _____ of his photograph. The mountains are stunning, and along with their reflection in the lake, are the first things you see. But if you look a little longer, you notice the forest on the **(3)** _____ and the cabin in the **(4)** _____ on the **(5)** _____.

This is a great **(6)** _____ of a young boy – it makes you wonder what he's thinking about. I really like the way that the trees in the **(7)** _____ are **(8)** _____ while the boy is **(9)** _____. It draws your attention to his face and his expression.

## 3 VOCABULARY: making comparisons

**Choose the correct options to complete the conversation.**

**Mario:** Which photo do you think I should submit for the photography competition?

**Lianne:** Wow, two completely different options!

**Mario:** Not totally – the photos are **(1)** similar in that / in contrast they are both portraits.

**Lianne:** Yes, that's true. But I think the **(2)** similarities / differences end there! Because the subject in this photo looks happy, **(3)** whereas / alike this woman looks so sad.

**Mario:** Which do you prefer?

**Lianne:** Well, I don't think the photo of the boy really grabs your attention, **(4)** alike / unlike the one of the woman, which is very intriguing. What's more, although the angle from which the photos are taken is **(5)** similar / difference, the photo of the woman is much more atmospheric.

**Mario:** That's interesting. Also, the background of the photograph of the woman is out of focus, **(6)** while / point of difference the photo of the boy is perfectly in focus. OK I've decided. I'm going to submit the one of the woman because I think the blurred background makes it more artistic.

**Lianne:** Good luck!

## 4 GRAMMAR: connectors of addition / cause and effect

**A  Match the two parts to make complete sentences.**

1  Connectors of addition are used to …
2  Connectors of cause and effect are used to …

a)  show how one thing makes another happen, or how one thought follows logically from another.
b)  add further points or to provide more information in support of a point.

**B  For each connector, write A (addition) or C (cause and effect).**

1  also ___
2  and ___
3  as a result of ___
4  besides that ___
5  as a consequence ___
6  moreover ___
7  because ___

8  due to ___
9  in addition to ___
10  therefore ___
11  so ___
12  because of ___
13  furthermore ___

**C  Choose the correct options to complete the text.**

29th August by Joanne Tanner                          8 comments
**Blog question: Is thinner always better?**

Share   Report   Comment                              Next post ▶

### Weight loss apps: Do they really work?

The current craze for selfies seems to be having an effect on body image **(1)** so / because people are constantly comparing themselves to their peers. **(2)** Due to, / As a consequence, we've seen the emergence of new apps, which have been designed to take 5 or 6 kg off your weight in photographs. **(3)** Moreover, / So, I decided to take a look at one of these apps myself so that I could see what all the hype was about. I installed the app and then I took a quick picture of myself **(4)** also / because the app only works on selfies. I decided to see what I would look like if I was 5 kg lighter – the results were not good. I looked ill **(5)** besides that / because of my incredibly thin face. My cheekbones were too sharp and my forehead looked huge. **(6)** In addition to / As a consequence that, my ears were out of proportion with my face! **(7)** Moreover, / Therefore, I can guarantee that thinner is NOT always better and I have since deleted the app from my phone!

### WHAT'S RIGHT?

Ⓧ  Lots of people want to be thinner as a result selfies.

✓  _____
_____
_____

## 5 COMMUNICATION STRATEGY: making comparisons

**A  Match the two parts to make complete sentences.**

1  In the first photo, the subject is smiling, …
2  Both photos are alike …
3  The first photo looks professional, …
4  Another point of difference is …
5  The first photo is very bright but …
6  The photos are similar in that …
7  The first photo was taken in a city, …
8  One similarity is that both …

a)  photos were taken outside.
b)  whereas in the second the subject looks serious.
c)  the angle from which the photo was taken.
d)  unlike the second, which was taken in a forest.
e)  while the second looks like an amateur effort.
f)  because they both show people playing sports.
g)  both were taken during the day.
h)  in contrast, the second is dark.

**B  Write the paired sentence numbers and letters from Exercise A in the correct place.**

1  To explain a similarity between two things: _____, _____, _____
2  To explain a difference between two things: _____, _____, _____, _____

**C** 🎧 **26** Listen to a man comparing the two photographs. Write *S* if he describes a similarity and *D* if he describes a difference.

1 ___      4 ___
2 ___      5 ___
3 ___      6 ___

## 6 GRAMMAR: verb + gerund/infinitive with a change in meaning

**A** Match the sentences (1–10) to their correct definitions of the words in bold (a–j).

1 I **forgot to turn** the lights out.
2 I **forgot meeting** her last summer.
3 We **regret to inform** you that the plane is delayed.
4 Sue **regrets introducing** her boyfriend to her parents.
5 I must **remember to buy** a present for my mother.
6 Do you **remember buying** this coat?
7 Should we **stop to have** lunch?
8 I'm going to **stop eating** chocolate in January.
9 I'll **try turning** it off and see if that works.
10 I'll **try to get** an A in my exam.

a) attempt sth. you may or may not be able to do
b) wish you hadn't done sth. in the past
c) not remember sth. you have to do
d) stop so that you can then do sth. else
e) have a memory of sth.
f) feel bad about something you have to tell sb.
g) not have a memory of sth.
h) do sth. to see what result it will have
i) stop an action or a habit
j) not forget something you have to do

**B** Choose the correct options to complete these sentences.

1 We regret to inform / informing you that your package has been lost.
2 I'm going to stop to drive / driving to work and will take the bus instead.
3 Chris remembered to meet / meeting the man before but he couldn't remember his name.
4 They forgot to reply / replying to the invitation and now it's too late.
5 I'll try to fix / fixing your car for you if you'd like.
6 I must remember to buy / buying a birthday card for Pete today.
7 Hannah regrets to eat / eating so much cake because now she feels sick.
8 If you want to get fit, why don't you try to swim / swimming?
9 I'll never forget to see / seeing the Eiffel Tower for the first time.
10 Lara stopped to get / getting some petrol for her car on her way home.

### WHAT'S RIGHT?

✗ I forgot handing in my assignment this morning.

✓ _____
_____

# SkillsStudio

**A**  Read the article about how camera phones are affecting photography.
Do the photographers who were interviewed for the article think that the
changes are having a positive or a negative effect on photography?

1  Antonio Olmos         positive / negative
2  Eamonn McCabe         positive / negative
3  Nick Knight           positive / negative

**B**  Choose the correct definitions of these underlined phrases in the article.

1  make someone redundant (paragraph A)
   a)  make somebody irrelevant
   b)  make somebody angry
2  scrap heap (paragraph A)
   a)  place where things are recycled
   b)  people or things who are no longer useful
3  become obsolete (paragraph B)
   a)  no longer used
   b)  come back into fashion
4  revolution in (paragraph B)
   a)  overthrow of the government
   b)  drastic change in ways of thinking

5  blow it up (paragraph B)
   a)  make something bigger
   b)  make something explode
6  a scattergun approach (to photography) (paragraph C)
   a)  take as many pictures as possible and hope that
       a few of them will be good
   b)  take pictures of people using guns
7  of choice (paragraph D)
   a)  generally preferred
   b)  a mixture of
8  be engaged by (paragraph D)
   a)  promise to marry
   b)  be interested in

**C**  Choose paragraphs A–E to answer the questions. You may use each
paragraph more than once.

Which paragraph(s) ...

- discusses methods of training photographers?  `1` ☐

- mention how photography has become more
  accessible for everyone?  `2` ☐ , ☐

- talks about how people are taking photos rather
  than experiencing events?  `3` ☐

- suggests that taking a lot of photos means that you
  always end up with a few good pictures?  `4` ☐

- compare the current situation in photography to
  something that happened in the past?  `5` ☐ , ☐

- discuss the quality of iPhone images?  `6` ☐ , ☐

- compare digital images to prints?  `7` ☐ , ☐

- states that photographers are no longer necessary?  `8` ☐

**D**  Write an opinion essay of
about 300 words with the title,
'There have never been so
many photographs taken, but
photography is dying.' Do you
agree?

# The death of photography:
# Are camera phones destroying an art form?

From presidential selfies to never-ending Instagram feeds, the world is now drowning in images. Celebrated photographers discuss the impact of this on their craft.

**A** 'It's really weird,' says 50-year-old award-winning Mexican photographer Antonio Olmos. 'Photography has never been so popular but it's getting destroyed. There have never been so many photographs taken but photography is dying. People taking photographs of their food in a restaurant instead of eating it. People taking photographs of the Mona Lisa instead of looking at it. I think the iPhone is taking people away from their experiences.' But what does Olmos mean by saying photography is dying? He argues that in the 1850s the rise of photography <u>made many painters</u>, who had previously made nice livings from painting family portraits, <u>redundant</u>. Now it's the turn of professional photographers to join the <u>scrap heap</u>. 'Photographers are getting destroyed by the rise of iPhones. Increasingly we don't need photographers – we can do just as well ourselves.'

**B** But doesn't that mean that some photographers are <u>becoming obsolete</u>, rather than that photography itself is dying? Isn't what we're witnessing a <u>revolution</u> in photography, thanks to digital technology, that makes it more democratic? 'In one sense yes,' says Olmos. 'I used to be sent on assignment to Iraq, Afghanistan – partly because there weren't any local photographers. Now thanks to digital technology, there are locals taking images at least as good as I can.' But there's a stronger reason that makes Olmos argue photography is dying. 'The iPhone has a poor-quality lens. You can take a beautiful picture on the iPhone and <u>blow it up</u> for a print and it looks terrible.' But who needs prints in a paper-free world? 'For me the print is the ultimate expression of photography,' he retorts. 'When I do street photography courses, I get people to print pictures – often for the first time. The idea is to slow them down, to make them make – not just take – photographs.'

**C** *Guardian* photographer Eamonn McCabe agrees: 'I think there's a depth to a print you don't get with digital.' Furthermore, he thinks that digital photography is lazy. Why? Because 'it's <u>a scattergun approach</u>. You snap away thinking, "One of these shots will work," rather than concentrate on capturing the image.' McCabe used to take two rolls of 24 exposures on a typical assignment. 'Now I can shoot 1000 pictures in one of these sessions on digital. I don't think photography's dead, it's just become lazy. People are taking lots of pictures but nobody's looking at them.'

**D** For a more positive sense of what digital and camera phone technology has done to photography, I speak to Nick Knight, the British fashion photographer who's just done two big assignments entirely on iPhone. 'I work frequently on the iPhone. It's almost become my camera <u>of choice</u>.' Indeed, Knight reckons that the current revolution in photography is as radical as what happened in the 1960s when fashion photographer David Bailey got rid of his tripod and started using a handheld camera. 'It gave him freedom and changed artistically what photography was. The same is true for me with the iPhone.' But what about the poor-quality iPhone lens? 'Who cares? The image isn't sharp? Big deal! One of my favourite photographers is Robert Capa, whose pictures are a bit blurry sometimes – I love them because he's captured a moment.' What Knight <u>is</u> also <u>engaged by</u> is how photography has become truly democratic. 'When I was a kid there was just one camera per family, if that. Now everybody has one and uses it all the time. That's great.' But why? Knight has been researching images of punk bands lately. 'There are hardly any images and all of them are from on stage. Compare that with now – at a Kanye West gig you see a sea of cameras, and there's a database of images.'

**E** But doesn't this democratisation of the medium threaten established photographers? Not necessarily. 'I'll survive in this profession because I have skills,' says Olmos. 'I'm a storyteller in images; my compositions are better than most people's. Just because you've got a microprocessor in your computer doesn't make you a writer. And just because you've got an Instagram app on your phone, you aren't a great photographer.'

*Adapted from* http://www.theguardian.com

# UNIT 12  BRIGHT LIGHTS, BIG CITY

## 1 GRAMMAR:  connectors of contrast

**A**  🎧 **27 Listen and complete the sentences.**

1  ☐ Rio was great _____ we didn't get to visit Sugarloaf Mountain.
2  ☐ I love travelling for pleasure _____ I really don't enjoy business travel.
3  ☐ _____ it was very crowded we enjoyed visiting the Louvre Museum in Paris.
4  ☐ London was a lot of fun _____ that it rained almost every day.
5  ☐ We decided to go to Shanghai _____ not speaking any Chinese.
6  ☐ Things have cost a little more than we'd expected _____ we've had a fantastic holiday.

**B**  Tick the sentences in Exercise A that have correct punctuation. Correct the incorrect sentences.

**C**  Complete the text with the correct connectors of contrast. Sometimes more than one answer is possible. You may use the connectors more than once.

> although   despite   even though   however   in spite of   nevertheless

# NORTH VIETNAM – HANOI
*Introducing Hanoi*   ASIA

### Hanoi walking tour, day 1: The Old Quarter

(1) _____ the noise and the pollution, Vietnam's capital city is a wonderful place to visit. In fact, it's worth visiting for the food alone! (2) _____, you can do more than just eat in this great city. (3) _____ you probably don't speak Vietnamese, it is easy to visit and enjoy many sights. The best place to start your day is in the Old Quarter. The market stalls open for breakfast at around 6am. (4) _____ you may not be used to having soup for breakfast, you should try the typical Vietnamese breakfast of *pho* – noodle soup flavoured with meat. (5) _____, if that doesn't sound good to you, then you can always get some delicious French bread. After breakfast, start your shopping on Lo Su Street. (6) _____ the fact that the narrow street is filled with motorbikes and crowds of people, it's a wonderful place to experience the real Vietnam. And (7) _____ you may not need anything new, you'll probably find a lot of things you want to buy. (8) _____, remember that it all has to fit in your suitcase!

## 2 VOCABULARY:  formal letters

Complete the phrases with the words from the box. Then match the phrases (1–6) to the correct functions (a–f).

> concerning   Dear   disappointed   Furthermore   hearing   Yours faithfully

1  We were very _____ with …
2  _____ Sir/Madam,
3  First of all, … _____, … Finally, …
4  I look forward to _____ from you.
5  I am writing _____ …
6  _____, Mrs EP Ruskin

a)  open a letter
b)  say why you're writing
c)  say that you didn't like something
d)  list your main complaints
e)  ask the person to reply
f)  close your letter

## 3 WRITING: a letter of complaint

### A Number the parts of the letter in the correct order.

**A** ☐ For these reasons, I request a full refund of the cost of the tour. I enclose the tickets and a copy of my receipt for £70 as proof of payment.

**B** ☐ First of all, although your website says that the tour goes to the harbour, one of the city's main attractions, we did not go there. Instead we stopped at City Hall, which was a huge disappointment. Furthermore, we were supposed to stop for photographs, but the driver didn't stop. Finally, in spite of the fact that your website said the tour includes a three-course lunch, we weren't served lunch at all – only a bottle of water!

**C** ☐ Dear Sir/Madam,

**D** ☐ Yours faithfully,
   Joseph May

**E** ☐ I am writing concerning your river boat trip that my mother and I took last Saturday. We chose your tour, despite the high price, because it looked very pleasant on your website and was supposed to include all of the main city attractions. However, we were very disappointed with it for a number of reasons.

**River Boat Trip**
RECEIPT

25/09/2015
11.36
Operator: John

2x Adult tickets                    £70.00

Visa Debit

THANK YOU
ENJOY YOUR TRIP

River Boat Trip
River Boat Trip
TICKET NO: 15864
Friday
25th September 2015
Time of issue: 11.36:12
TICKET TYPE: Adult

TICKET NO: 15864

### B Match paragraphs A, B and E to their main purpose.

Paragraph A          a) the writer gives details of what he doesn't like
Paragraph B          b) the writer states what he wants
Paragraph E          c) the writer says he's writing to complain

### C Complete the letter of complaint with the phrases from the box.

Dear Sir/Madam   Finally   First of all   For these reasons   Furthermore   I am writing concerning
I enclose   I look forward to hearing from you   Yours faithfully   we were very disappointed with it

(1) _____,
(2) _____ my stay in your eco-lodge last month. My husband and I booked a room in your lodge, despite the high price, because it looked like a peaceful location with luxury comforts. However, (3) _____ for a number of reasons.
(4) _____, although your website clearly shows a picture of a swimming pool with people swimming in it, the pool had no water in it, so we couldn't swim. (5) _____, the food you served was very basic, but the website says you serve high-quality gourmet food. Also, in spite of the fact that you're supposed to be an eco-lodge, the room had disposable paper cups for tea and coffee, and they washed our towels every day. (6) _____, even though your website described your rooms as 'airy tree-house accommodation', our room was a small, dark building on the ground.
(7) _____, I believe you should refund 75% of the cost of our stay. (8) _____ some pictures of the empty pool, the dark room and one basic meal, and a copy of our receipt.
(9) _____.
(10) _____,
Mrs EP Ruskin

## 4 VOCABULARY: describing places

**A** Put the letters into the correct order to make words used to describe places.

1 redat _____
2 taher _____
3 wevis _____
4 eylal _____

5 theagier _____
6 laglive _____
7 eist _____
8 meltentest _____

**B** Complete the text with the correct form of the words from Exercise A.

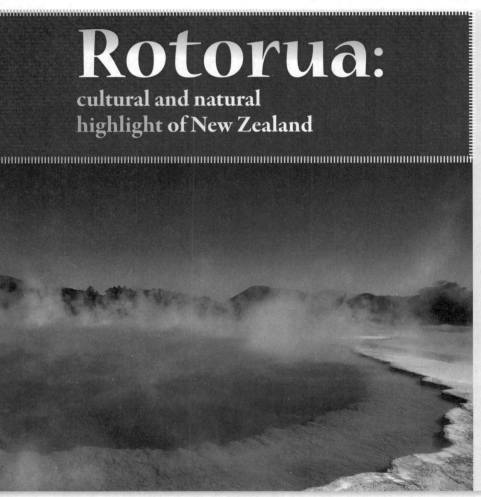

# Rotorua:
## cultural and natural
## highlight of New Zealand

The city of Rotorua is thought by many to be at the **(1)** _____ of traditional Māori culture in New Zealand. It was originally the **(2)** _____ of the Te Arawa Māori tribes who set up home here more than 600 years ago. The first Europeans arrived in the 1820s when **(3)** _____ with neighbouring areas began.

Today, Rotorua is one of New Zealand's most popular tourist destinations. Visitors come here to learn more about the rich **(4)** _____ of the Māori people. A highlight for many tourists is a visit to a traditional Māori **(5)** _____ or *pā* to experience how native people used to live before Rotorua grew into the modern city that it is today.

Rotorua is also a **(6)** _____ which experiences a lot of geothermal activity. From here tourists can enjoy **(7)** _____ over the breathtaking Waimangu Volcanic Valley or visit the hot springs and mud pools at Kuirau Park. However, Rotorua is not just famous for its stunning surroundings. It is well worth exploring the streets and **(8)** _____ of the city, which has been voted 'New Zealand's most beautiful' six times.

## 5 LISTENING: rapid speech

**A** 🎧 28 Listen and choose the correct option to complete the sentences.

1 Sarah and Danni are talking mostly about plans for the future / recent experiences.
2 Sarah talks mostly about work / travel.
3 Sarah mentions members of her family / her boyfriend several times.
4 Sarah and Danni discuss a local shop / library.

**B** Listen again. Answer the questions.

1 What country is Sarah going to visit? _____
2 What's she especially interested in? _____
3 What part of the city do Sarah's relatives live in? _____
4 What does she plan on learning while she's there? _____
5 What are Danni's plans for the summer? _____
6 What does Sarah suggest to Danni? _____

## 6 GRAMMAR: ways of talking about the future

**A** Match the sentence halves to make complete sentences.

1 Use *may, might* or *will*
2 Use *going to*
3 Use the present continuous
4 Use the future continuous

a) to talk about things that will be happening at a particular time in the future.
b) to make predictions about the future and talk about intentions.
c) to talk about arrangements and fixed plans.
d) to make predictions about the future.

**B** Choose the best options to complete the text.

### Lost cities of the future

Most people are fascinated by great lost cities like Peru's Machu Picchu, which was the religious heart of the great Inca Empire. We're equally fascinated by the reasons for their ruin. Often scientists can only guess what turned the great settlements of the past into today's mysterious archaeological sites. But some experts believe the great cities of today **(1) may be / are being** the lost cities of tomorrow and we won't be in any doubt about the causes.

One American city, New Orleans, was already nearly destroyed in 2005 by Hurricane Katrina and its future remains uncertain. Even as residents rebuild, many say they have a firm plan in the event of another hurricane: they **(2) might leave / are leaving** forever.

On the other side of the Atlantic, the historic city of Venice in Italy is also under threat – it has sunk by more than 60 cm since the 18th century as a result of rising sea levels. New flood gates are nearly finished and it is hoped that these **(3) will prevent / are preventing** flooding. However, in spite of these efforts, some experts believe that Venice **(4) will be sinking / may sink** another 8 cm by 2032.

Another city under threat from the sea is Bangkok in Thailand. Scientists believe that huge floods, such as those that engulfed the city in 2011, **(5) may become / are becoming** more common in the future. Also, some experts predict that Thailand **(6) is experiencing / will be experiencing** more frequent tropical cyclones and hurricanes in the years ahead.

Authorities in Shanghai, China, are also fighting a battle against rising sea levels. They currently pump 60,000 tonnes of water a year back into wells to prevent flooding in the city. In the near future they **(7) are going to build / are building** flood gates on the river, which **(8) is being / will be** reassuring for the 20 million people who live there.

### WHAT'S RIGHT?

ⓧ By the time this concert ends, the trains and buses won't run.

✓ _____
_____
_____

Information source: http://scribol.com/science/five-lost-cities-of-the-future

# SkillsStudio

**A  Match the headlines and the pictures.**

1 ___  Report states that Beijing air quality is 'major concern'

2 ___  Global warming may lead to wild bears in New York in 30 years

3 ___  UN report says urban population to hit 5 billion by 2030

4 ___  *Why we should be concerned about running out of oil*

**B  Which problems match each headline in Exercise A? Write the correct number(s).**

___ limited resources     ___ overcrowding     ___ climate change     ___ pollution

**C  ♪ 29 Listen to a student give a presentation about cities of the future.
Tick the problems she says cities will have to solve by 2050.**

☐ limited resources     ☐ overcrowding     ☐ climate change     ☐ pollution

**D Listen again. Choose the correct answer.**

1   A *dome* is a kind of …
   **a)** fan.       **b)** vehicle.      **c)** artificial cloud.      **d)** roof.

2   In the presentation, the word *address* means …
   **a)** deal with.      **b)** speak about.    **c)** a location.      **d)** a formal speech.

3   The student thinks cities of the future will have cleaner air because …
   **a)** there will be less traffic.
   **b)** cars will use better petrol.
   **c)** everyone will be driving electric cars.
   **d)** we will run out of oil to pollute the air with.

4   Why does the student mention traffic?
   **a)** to explain why pollution will increase in 2050
   **b)** to make a joke
   **c)** to give a reason why electric cars are better
   **d)** to consider an opposing argument

5   Why does the student think underwater cities might be possible?
   **a)** Because people in the US Navy have lived underwater since the 1960s.
   **b)** Because science fiction writers have shown that the idea could work.
   **c)** Because a new city is already being built underwater right now.
   **d)** Because there have already been successful experiments in underwater living.

**E Listen again. Tick the statements that the student would probably agree with.**

1   ☐ Scientists in the 1970s correctly predicted the problems cities would face.
2   ☐ Not every city today is perfect.
3   ☐ Cars are not the most important cause of air pollution.
4   ☐ There is enough oil on the planet to last for hundreds of years.
5   ☐ There is probably no way to reduce the population of cities.
6   ☐ It would be very pleasant to live on the moon.

**F How do you think the place where you live will be different in 2050? Write a presentation of about 200 words. Think of two problems your area faces. For each problem, describe the issue and explain how it may be solved in your area by 2050.**

# Audio script

## UNIT 1
### Track 02

**Mark:** Welcome to *Smart Talk*. I'm your host, Mark Owens. Today we're talking to Lisa Adams, an expert on parenting, who's just written a fascinating book on children and identity. Welcome, Dr Adams.

**Lisa:** Thank you, Mark.

**Mark:** Now, I wanted to ask you about your chapter on clothing and children's identities. You have some very interesting and, uh, unusual ideas here.

**Lisa:** Yes. A lot of parents don't want to buy their children cool clothes or designer brands because they think it will have a negative effect on their sense of identity.

**Mark:** And you disagree with that idea.

**Lisa:** Uh, yes and no. I mean, a child's identity should not be based on fashion. But at the same time, fashionable clothes make people look good, and if people look good, they feel good – even children. And kids need to be accepted by their social group. So I think it is good to buy cool clothes for your children, even when they're three or four years old.

**Mark:** I'm sorry, but I just don't think that's true. First of all, I think it's more important that children are comfortable and can run around and climb trees without worrying about what they look like, or damaging their expensive designer clothes. But more importantly, children shouldn't be worrying about their sense of style and social status, especially three-year-olds. It teaches them the wrong values, doesn't it?

**Lisa:** I'm afraid I can't agree. I think children have the right to wear designer clothes if their parents have enough money. I don't mean that children should have designer stuff worth two million pounds! But they have the right to look cool, if they want to.

**Mark:** In a sense, you're right: if the parents have a lot of money, why shouldn't they spend it on their kids' clothes? But I think it puts a lot of pressure on mums and dads to spend money that they don't necessarily have, so their children look cool.

**Lisa:** Well, yes, to a certain extent, but you know, there are non-designer brands that make cool kids' clothes.

**Mark:** Well, uh, that's true, but I just think that children should develop a sense of identity based on who they are, not what they wear.

**Lisa:** I couldn't agree more. But it's still important to look good at the same time, isn't it?

## UNIT 2
### Track 03

1 The thing about globalisation is how dependent we all are on one another economically. I mean, if there's some sort of natural disaster or something in one part of the world, then it'll affect the markets there. Then in the following days, you know, we'll feel the ripple effects of that in stock markets across the world. If prices fall dramatically in one country, then they are going to, like, crash everywhere.

2 The other night I called my insurance company in London because my roof started to leak during a storm. I thought I was speaking to someone in the UK but then, well, I realised I was talking to a woman in India. She was, like, helping me from the other side of the world. She was great. The best thing was that even though it was the middle of the night in the UK, I could still talk to someone because, you know, because of the time difference. It meant that the call centre was open and I could get it all sorted out right away.

3 Recently my neighbours bought a sofa from a local shop. The sofa was made overseas somewhere, but they were happy, you know, because it was really comfortable. Then they started getting these, kind of, weird burns on their legs. The doctors couldn't find the problem. Eventually the local shop announced that there was a dangerous chemical in the sofa and my neighbours got their money back. But that's not good enough. I mean, globalisation is fine, but if we buy and sell things around the world, we should all have the same standards.

4 I think globalisation's great! I love using social networking sites because, well, it kind of means that I have friends all over the world now. I have, like, 500 friends. It's really cool. I mean, they send me photographs, music, videos – all kinds of stuff from their countries – and, you know, I send them things from my country, too. It's amazing.

### Track 04

1 The thing about globalisation is how dependent we all are on one another economically. I mean, if there's some sort of natural disaster or something in one part of the world, then it'll affect the markets there. Then in the following days, you know, we'll feel the ripple effects of that in stock markets across the world. If prices fall dramatically in one country, then they are going to, like, crash everywhere.

2   The other night I called my insurance company in London because my roof started to leak during a storm. I thought I was speaking to someone in the UK, but then, well, I realised I was talking to a woman in India. She was, like, helping me from the other side of the world. She was great. The best thing was that even though it was the middle of the night in the UK, I could still talk to someone because, you know, because of the time difference. It meant that the call centre was open and I could get it all sorted out right away.

3   Recently my neighbours bought a sofa from a local shop. The sofa was made overseas somewhere, but they were happy, you know, because it was really comfortable. Then they started getting these, kind of, weird burns on their legs. The doctors couldn't find the problem. Eventually the local shop announced that there was a dangerous chemical in the sofa and my neighbours got their money back. But that's not good enough. I mean, globalisation is fine, but if we buy and sell things around the world, we should all have the same standards.

## Track 05

I think globalisation's great! I love using social networking sites because, well, it kind of means that I have friends all over the world now. I have, like, 500 friends. It's really cool. I mean, they send me photographs, music, videos – all kinds of stuff from their countries – and, you know, I send them things from my country, too. It's amazing.

## Track 06

1   support
2   promote
3   campaign
4   generate
5   value
6   sustain
7   participate
8   boost

## Track 07

John:   And now it's time for our weekly feature, *Let's Talk Travel*. And joining me in the studio today is Scott Williams, author of a brand new book called *Sustainable Travel*. He's here to speak to us about ethical tourism. Welcome to the show, Scott.

Scott:  Thanks for inviting me, John. It's great to be here.

John:   So, Scott, tell us, what is an ethical tourist exactly?

Scott:  Well, an ethical tourist is a traveller who does everything possible to make sure that the impact that they have on the local environment, culture and people of the country is positive and not negative.

John:   Oh, OK. I see. So how can countries be affected negatively by tourism?

Scott:  Well, for a start, tourism can be harmful to the environment. With globalisation, there are more aeroplanes flying around the planet than ever before, which means increased carbon emissions. I read somewhere that there are something like 93,000 flights every day!

John:   Wow, that's certainly a lot of carbon in the air …

Scott:  It is. And by now, we all know the dangers of global warming … But it's not just that. Tourists sometimes ruin some of the most beautiful and remote areas of the world because they leave rubbish behind them, which can be really hard to get rid of. And the demands of tourism can also sometimes threaten the limited natural resources of an area, such as water. For example, an average-sized golf course can use more than half a million gallons of water EVERY SINGLE DAY. Some areas just don't have enough water to sustain that sort of demand.

John:   Yes, I see … And are there any other problems that can be caused by tourism?

Scott:  Oh, definitely. Tourism can sometimes harm local communities.

John:   Really? That surprises me. Why is that? I mean, surely tourism is good for local communities, isn't it? It generates jobs and boosts the local economy. A lot of people depend on the tourism trade, don't they?

Scott:  Yes, that's true. But, unfortunately, the tourism market is often dominated by multinational companies and, in some places, regional businesses just can't compete with the prices. And what's more, sometimes local people are forced to leave their homes to make way for tourism developments …

John:   That's awful. So, what can we do about it? How can we all become ethical tourists?

Scott:  Well, there are all kinds of things we can do. For a start, wherever possible, we should use ethical transportation – like the train, boat or even a bike.

John:   I hear what you're saying, Scott. But are you being realistic? It's not always possible to do that, is it? For example most people only have a few days holiday a year – if they want to visit Vietnam, they don't have time to take a boat!

**Scott:** No, that's true. But there are other ways that we can play a role in helping the environment – for example, we can leave any excess packaging at home. Remember that some countries don't have the waste facilities to deal with our rubbish.

**John:** Yes, that's a good idea. What else can we do?

**Scott:** Well, make sure you find out about the ethics of your tour operator before you hand over your money. An ethical company will be more than willing to share information about subjects such as whether they pay their local employees a fair wage, for example. Just be conscious of the fact that some operators care more about making money than helping local people.

**John:** I'm sorry but I'm going to have to stop you there, Scott, because we're running out of time. Thank you so much for coming in to talk to us today …

## UNIT 3

### Track 08

Conversation 1
A: Hey, have you read the new Stephen King novel?
B: No, it's not really my thing.
A: You should read it. It's really creepy. I couldn't put it down!

Conversation 2
A: Muhammad Ali is one of the greatest people ever.
B: Do you really think so? What about Gandhi and Martin Luther King, Jr.? As great as them?

Conversation 3
A: I think it's horrible that so many young people just want to be famous.
B: What do you mean?

Conversation 4
A: I think friendship must be really hard for famous people.
B: No way! Famous people all have lots of friends. Other famous people!

Conversation 5
A: I don't know why Kanye West got together with Kim Kardashian. He's so talented, but she … well, you know.
B: So you're saying you don't think she has talent?

Conversation 6
A: Anyone can break a world record and become famous.
B: Oh, yeah, right. So you're going to run a marathon in two hours and the world will know your name?

### Track 09

Conversation 1
A: Hey, have you read the new Stephen King novel?
B: No, it's not really my thing.
A: You should read it. It's really creepy. I couldn't put it down!
B: Maybe I'm not making myself clear. I don't read horror books at all. They're too scary for me!

Conversation 2
A: Muhammad Ali is one of the greatest people ever.
B: Do you really think so? What about Gandhi and Martin Luther King, Jr.? As great as them?
A: Well, perhaps I should rephrase that – he's one of the greatest athletes ever.

Conversation 3
A: I think it's horrible that so many young people just want to be famous.
B: What do you mean?
A: Talent used to come first, put it that way. In the past, kids wanted to be famous for being good at something. Now they just want fame!

Conversation 4
A: I think friendship must be really hard for famous people.
B: No way! Famous people all have lots of friends. Other famous people!
A: What I'm trying to say is, fame makes it hard for famous people to maintain relationships with non-celebrities because their lives are so different.

Conversation 5
A: I don't know why Kanye West got together with Kim Kardashian. He's so talented, but she … well, you know.
B: So you're saying you don't think she has talent?
A: Actually, that's not what I meant. She's got some talent. She's good at promoting herself. But he's just so much more talented.

Conversation 6
A: Anyone can break a world record and become famous.
B: Oh, yeah, right. So you're going to run a marathon in two hours and the world will know your name?
A: Well, what I meant was, you can come up with your own idea, like sitting in a tree for the longest time or something, and then do it, and you get famous!

## UNIT 4

### Track 10

Australia is officially the happiest country in the world for the fourth year running. That's according to the Better Life Index, which is put together each year by the Organisation for Economic Cooperation and Development (the OECD). In general, it's not easy to measure well-being. As a result, the OECD ranks their 36 member countries according to 11 different criteria. They consider things that affect material living conditions. These include housing, income and jobs. In addition, they look at features that influence the quality of life – these are community, environment, education, civic engagement, health, safety, life satisfaction and work-life balance.

So far 60,000 people have taken part in the research, sharing their views about each of these areas. What's more, people are able to state which criteria are most important to them. To a great extent, the most important factor for people's happiness is life satisfaction, closely followed by health and education.

Scandinavia dominates the top 5 with Norway, Sweden, and Denmark at numbers 2, 3, and 4 respectively; furthermore, Finland comes in at number 8. On the other hand, towards the lower end of the list is Greece, whose citizens have the lowest life satisfaction, and as a consequence they came in at number 34. That said, it's not all bad news. Greece reports above average health and quality of environment. Mexico is in 35$^{th}$ place – on the whole there is a high level of life satisfaction but safety is a significant issue. Turkey ranks poorly for income and housing, and consequently it came in at 36$^{th}$ place. Nevertheless, Turkey is praised for improving the quality of life for citizens over the last 20 years.

### Track 11

1  pessimistic
2  depressed
3  state of well-being
4  optimistic
5  in a good mood
6  distracted
7  emotions
8  focused

### Track 12

**Susie:** Hey, Grandpa, I'm reading this article about the ages when people are happiest.

**Ron:** Really? And when are people happiest?

**Susie:** Well, according to a recent report, our happiness peaks twice in our lives. The first peak is when we're 23. I'm almost 24! Does that mean it's all downhill from here? That's depressing. Do you agree with that? Were you happiest at 23?

**Ron:** Well, I was very happy at that age, yes. At 23 you're young and optimistic about life. You have a lot of expectations about what lies ahead. In addition, you don't have any of the responsibilities or worries that you have later in life. And life is fun and full of possibility.

**Susie:** Well, I suppose I'd better make the most of it and appreciate every moment then! Anyway, the article says that when you're 23, you overestimate your future life satisfaction by an average of about 10%. Then over the next few decades, you begin to feel more and more disappointed about life until you hit a low point in your mid-50s.

**Ron:** Oh, why is that? What is it about your mid-50s that's so bad?

**Susie:** It says that's the age when you have the strongest feeling of regret because you realise that the dreams you had when you were younger aren't going to come true.

**Ron:** Hmm, I don't agree with that at all. When you're in your 50s, there's still time to pursue your dreams.

**Susie:** Oh, yes. That's right. You had a career change at about that stage of your life, didn't you?

**Ron:** Yes, I quit my job in sales when I was 53 and retrained as a yoga instructor. It was the best move I ever made – I may not have been as wealthy after that but at least I had a job that I enjoyed. And I was much, much more content than I had ever been before. So, what does it say about after the age of 55?

**Susie:** Well, interestingly, that's when satisfaction levels start to rise again as you accept the disappointments in your life. Then, your state of well-being peaks when you reach the age of 69.

**Ron:** Hmm, why 69, I wonder?

**Susie:** Well, it says that 68-year-olds underestimate their future happiness by 4.5%, so maybe that's why. As you get older, you have lower expectations about life, so you have fewer disappointments, and so consequently you feel more content.

**Ron:** Now, that I do agree with. As you get older, your expectations do change. So, what happens after 69?

**Susie:** Hmm. It says satisfaction levels decline after 75 …

**Ron:** Well, bearing in mind that I'm almost 80, that hasn't put me in a good mood! I hate to say it but, on the whole, I agree with that. I get frustrated these days that I can't do what I used to in spite of all the yoga I've done over the years! I'd be interested to know more about that report though. Do you know how many people they spoke to and what backgrounds they came from? Because I think it's very hard to generalise about happiness.

**Susie:** Hmm, hang on. It says here somewhere … oh, yes. Here it is. It was based on German data from more than 23,161 individuals, between the ages of 17 and 85. And they spoke to people from all over Germany, and the results that they got were similar in spite of the economic and cultural differences between the regions.

**Ron:** Hmm, that's interesting. Maybe there is something to it then …

## UNIT 5
### Track 13

**A:** Should we order a bottle of water for the table?

**B:** Maybe. Uh, how much does it cost?

**A:** Let's see. They range from three to six pounds a bottle.

**B:** Three pounds? It would have to be a big bottle to make it worth that much.

**A:** It's no more expensive than a soft drink. And it tastes better than tap water.

**B:** Really? I bet if tap water was put up against bottled water in a taste test, you wouldn't be able to tell the difference!

**A:** Of course I would!

**B:** Hmm. Maybe, but for me it's as much about the environment as it is the price. Those plastic bottles are bad for the planet. They really shouldn't market bottled water as something clean and healthy, you know.

**A:** But it makes me feel healthy!

**B:** But bottled water IS bad for the environment, AND it's too expensive.

**A:** OK, OK! Let's just get tap water!

### Track 14

**Sadia:** Look at this. What can we do to raise awareness about water pollution?

**Tom:** We could try collecting some rubbish from the river and displaying it.

**Sadia:** I like that idea! I'd suggest putting it on display by the river.

**Tom:** Maybe, but the rubbish might fall into the river again. What about displaying it somewhere indoors? There's always the school.

**Jess:** No, not the school. Since adult shoppers throw most of the rubbish in the river, let's focus on them. Have you considered giving the shopping centre a try?

**Tom:** Nice idea, but I don't think it would accept the rubbish. Hey, what if we take photos of the rubbish instead? We could display photos in the shopping centre.

**Jess:** Or another option would be to hand out leaflets.

### Track 15
#### Interview 1

**Interviewer:** Hello, I'm doing a survey about weddings. I wonder if you could spare a moment to share your views on the subject. Do you think weddings are an important ritual in society?

**Speaker 1:** Well, I guess weddings are important but they cost so much money these days. People are under a lot of pressure to organise the perfect event. You've got the new clothes, the venue, the food, the flowers, not to mention the honeymoon. I mean it can end up costing thousands of pounds. And sometimes it's the young couple that has to pay for it all. Quite frankly, I think that young people have better things to spend their money on, like saving to buy a house. After all, a wedding only lasts for one day but a house lasts a lifetime, right?

#### Interview 2

**Speaker 2:** Yes, definitely. I love going to weddings. They're just wonderful. Everyone wears amazing clothes, too. It's the one day of your life when you get to be a star with all of your friends and family. The other thing is – and I know this is really old-fashioned – but I think it's important for people to be serious about being together, you know? It's a big step and it's important to mark the occasion.

#### Interview 3

**Speaker 3:** Well, I have to confess that I don't really like going to traditional weddings! I mean, weddings are an important ritual and all, but I just find them boring sometimes. When I was young, weddings were all the same. The man wore a dark suit. The woman wore a white dress. But nowadays, you can have it any way you want and you have so much more choice. So a wedding is important not because it's traditional, but because you can do it your own way – barefoot on the beach, jumping out of a plane – anything goes.

Interview 4

Speaker 4: Well, getting married is important, but I don't think the wedding ceremony part of it is that important. I believe that people are just wasting their money – and mine! I went to five weddings last year and I spent a fortune on presents. I'm tired of going to weddings now. You know, I'm all for love and I'm happily married myself but it's just crazy to spend tens of thousands of pounds on one party.

## Track 16

1 fresher
2 initiation
3 mascot
4 high-ranking
5 ritual
6 symbolic

## Track 17

1 One of the most unusual festivals in my country, Thailand, is the Monkey Buffet Festival, which is held in Lopburi. The area is full of monkeys and, once a year, the villagers hold a picnic in their honour. Over 600 monkeys enjoy grilled sausage, fresh fruit, ice cream and other monkey treats! Monkeys are traditionally treated with respect in Thailand, but having said that, the Monkey Buffet Festival is not a tradition that dates back very far. It was started in 1989 by a local hotel owner – to be honest, I think the motivation for setting up this tradition may have been more about promoting tourism rather than honouring wildlife. It has certainly boosted tourism in the region because the festival gets bigger and better each year, pulling in lots of visitors hoping to catch sight of this unusual festivity.

2 The most unusual festival in my country is the annual Cheese-Rolling Festival, which is held every May in Gloucester in the west of England – basically a large round of cheese is rolled down a hill, and the competitors race down to see who can catch it. The person who catches the cheese gets to take it home! Nobody is quite sure where this tradition comes from but it's at least 200 years old. Some think it used to be a fertility ritual to encourage a big harvest and others say it was what people used to have to do to maintain their right to use the land for their animals. But, to be honest, nowadays it's just an excuse to turn up and have a good laugh!

3 The highlight of the festival calendar in Spain for me is La Tomatina (that's L-A T-O-M-A-T-I-N-A), which is held on the last Wednesday of August every year in the town of Buñol near Valencia. It's basically the biggest food fight in the world! It's such good fun – over the course of exactly one hour, we hurl 100 tons of overripe tomatoes at each other! The festival started in about 1944 and it seems to get bigger each year. Just recently, the town has started to sell entry tickets to cover the costs of the event. I guess it's fair enough really – you can just imagine what the streets look like by the end and the fire engines have to clean up using fire hoses.

4 There's a great festival on the island of Shetland, in Scotland called Up Helly Aa. It's a fire festival to mark the end of winter where the local people dress up as Vikings and parade through the town at night with torches. At the end of the parade everyone sets fire to a ship called a galley. Then the parade splits into groups and they do comedy or entertaining acts at different venues around the town. It's a fascinating spectacle to watch and the night really generates a strong feeling of community. You should definitely look it up online. It's spelled U-P, new word, H-E-L-L-Y, new word, A-A.

5 An unusual ritual in my country, Japan, is Konaki Sumo (that's K-O-N-A-K-I, new word, S-U-M-O). What happens is two Sumo wrestlers face each other and each of them holds a baby, also facing forward. The winner is the baby who starts to cry first. And if both babies start to cry at the same time, then the winner is the one who cries the loudest. It may sound strange but we have this old proverb, 'crying babies grow fast', because we believe that the louder a baby cries the more the gods have blessed it. It's a ritual that's at least 400 years old and it gives us a chance to be grateful for the babies' health.

## UNIT 8

## Track 18

Jim: I want to paint the kitchen and I was hoping we could talk about the colours.

Nick: OK. I was thinking we might choose a neutral colour, like cream.

Jim: Oh, really? I wanted to suggest using something more exciting.

Nick: More exciting? Like what?

Jim: I was wondering if we should paint it orange and red.

Nick: Orange and red?! I'm not sure that's the best idea. Those colours don't really work with the table and chairs.

Jim: Oh, I see what you mean. Maybe cream is best, after all.

## Track 19

1 poverty
2 ambassador
3 philanthropic
4 humanitarian
5 refugee
6 injustice
7 underprivileged
8 foundation

## Track 20

### Part 1

In today's lecture we'll be looking at the movement to eradicate poverty through market-based solutions. We'll be focusing on a pioneering company, now called Ten Thousand Villages, which began the fair trade movement. First, a bit of background information. Ten Thousand Villages is a non-profit charitable fair trade organisation that buys the handcrafted products it sells, for example, jewellery, items for the home, toys, games, baskets, stationery and so on, direct from the producers. And, being a fair trade company, all of their products are bought at a fair price. The products are sold through a retail network of over seventy shops – mostly in shopping centres – and online. The company also sells a number of products to hundreds of other retailers throughout the USA, and they sell direct to customers at festivals, usually hosted by community groups, churches or colleges.

### Part 2

Now let's move on to the company's history. It all started when an American named Edna Ruth Byler visited Puerto Rico in 1946. While there, she met a number of women artisans. She was impressed with their work, but she was shocked by the poverty in which they lived and wanted to take action to help them. Following that trip, Byler started an organisation called the Overseas Needlepoint and Crafts Project that bought the products for a fair price and sold them in the North American market. For the next thirty years, she worked to help artisans in developing countries – for example, Cambodia, the Philippines, Uganda and countless others – to sell their products at fair prices in the USA. The business became extremely successful and improved the lives of thousands of artisans and their families who had been living in poverty. Byler retired in 1979 but others continued her work.

### Part 3

Now, let's turn our attention to its more recent history. In 1996, the organisation celebrated its 50th birthday. It changed its name to Ten Thousand Villages, and in 1997, it opened the first Ten Thousand Villages store. Prior to that, the products had been sold to other organisations and retailers. Then in 2006, the company began selling its products online, which has proved to be a huge success. Recently, Ten Thousand Villages has been named one of the world's most ethical companies by Forbes Magazine and the Ethisphere Institute. And the company's vision continues to be that no artisan will be exploited.

Now, I'd like to look in some detail at exactly where …

## Track 21

**Sophia:** Welcome back, you're listening to Radio 35 *Daily Debate* with me, Sophia Peters. Next, we're going to talk about celebrity humanitarians and whether they do more harm than good. I'm joined in the studio today by two guests – journalist Paul Cunard and Nahla Simons, who is a representative of the Kitts Humanitarian Foundation. Thank you both for joining us today.

**Paul:** It's a pleasure.

**Nahla:** Good to be here.

**Sophia:** OK, Paul, let's start with you – you've recently written a very passionate article called 'Celebrity do-gooders do more harm than good'. Tell us more.

**Paul:** Well, I just don't buy into the whole celebrity humanitarian thing, I'm afraid. We've all heard about celebrities doing their bit for charities. But in my opinion, the only reason that celebrities get involved in charity work is to promote themselves and raise their profiles. They pretend to be helping the poor but really they are just making themselves richer.

**Sophia:** Nahla, I can see you shaking your head. Would you like to join in here?

**Nahla:** Yes, I would. I don't think it's helpful to make such broad generalisations about people's motivations – some of these people are just trying to use their profiles to raise awareness about issues that they care about.

**Paul:** I'm sorry, Nahla, but I think you're being a little naïve.

**Nahla:** No, I'm not. Just because a person is rich or famous doesn't mean they aren't allowed to feel a sense of social responsibility. Maybe they feel it even more strongly because they have so much, whereas others have so little. How can you be so sure that their intentions are bad?

**Paul:** Well, the facts speak for themselves. It's all about money. For example, the Live 8 concerts in 2005 turned out to be great marketing for the corporate sponsors. And the artists who generously gave their time for free got to play to the whole world and some had increased sales of up to 3600% in the week after the concerts. Frankly, I don't think it had much to do with getting governments to make promises about global poverty.

**Nahla:** OK, I hear what you're saying. But the good that celebrity ambassadors can do for a charity far outweighs the negatives that you are highlighting. You can't deny that people like Angelina Jolie, George Clooney and Bono have made an enormous contribution to humanitarian efforts. And, in my experience, charity organisations are delighted when they receive support from well-known faces because a celebrity endorsement usually raises a charity's profile, which means that they get more donations from the public.

**Paul:** I appreciate that, but the worrying thing is that celebrities tend to focus attention and resources on short-term, media-friendly crises, which means that we end up dealing with the symptoms rather than the causes of the problems. The media focus on the dramatic pictures of children crying and destroyed houses, without dealing with the main issues of social inequality.

**Sophia:** Nahla, would you like to respond to that?

**Nahla:** Yes, I would. I couldn't disagree more. What about Ben Affleck's Eastern Congo Initiative? That's not a short-term reaction to a crisis. He founded this initiative a few years ago and it helps to fund local Congolese-led programmes to build safe and sustainable communities for the future.

**Paul:** I see your point, Nahla. Maybe there are a few exceptions to the rule but generally, I think we're just going to have to agree to disagree on this …

**Sophia:** And I'm afraid that I'm going to have to stop you there, Paul, because we've run out of time. Thank you both for coming in and talking to us today. We like nothing more than a lively discussion here at *Daily Debate*.

## UNIT 9
### Track 22

**A:** Here's an interesting article. It's all about how to win at 'Rock, Paper, Scissors'.

**B:** That's ridiculous. There's no skill or strategy for the game.

**A:** Well, maybe. The article says many people think that winning or losing in 'Rock, Paper, Scissors' is mostly about luck.

**B:** Exactly.

**A:** Let me finish. But actually, you can use strategies to win.

**B:** OK, like what, for example?

**A:** Here's one. Statistics show that players with less experience usually begin a game by playing the 'rock' gesture.

**B:** Really? There are studies on this?

**A:** That's what it says. Anyway, that's why you should always start with paper against an inexperienced player.

**B:** Because your opponent is probably going to play rock and paper beats rock.

**A:** Exactly.

**B:** That's fine but what if my opponent already knows about that strategy?

**A:** Simple. You should play scissors first to beat experienced players because they'll know the tactic and will begin with paper.

**B:** All right, I can believe that. What else does it say?

**A:** It says you have a good opportunity to win if the person you're playing against makes the same gesture twice.

**B:** Oh, why is that?

**A:** Well, the other player will probably make a different gesture the third time because they think this will be more difficult to predict.

**B:** And isn't it?

**A:** Actually no, Let's say the other person plays paper and then paper again. The third time, they'll probably do rock or scissors.

**B:** Not paper.

**A:** Exactly. So you can play rock. You might win, you might tie, but you won't lose.

**B:** I never thought of that!

## UNIT 10
### Track 23

1 be exposed to
2 dare to
3 failure
4 freedom
5 play it safe
6 risky
7 security
8 take a chance

## Track 24

**Jenny:** Hey Mae, did you hear that they've closed off the recreation area in the park?

**Mae:** No, why did they do that?

**Jenny:** Well, apparently, a boy fell off the slide and broke his arm, so I guess they must have decided that it's unsafe.

**Mae:** You've got to be kidding. People are just too overprotective these days.

**Jenny:** You're right; it's kind of extreme. But I think parents just want to keep their kids safe.

**Mae:** Well, I think that children need to take risks in order to learn how to manage risks.

**Jenny:** Oh, I don't know about that. If I had kids, I wouldn't want them playing in a park where somebody had broken their arm.

**Mae:** But accidents can happen anywhere. That kid could have fallen out of bed and broken his arm! Children learn basic survival skills through play, and if we don't let them take risks when they are young, then they won't know how to handle them when they grow up.

**Jenny:** Hmm, you've got a point there.

## Track 25

**Jane:** Good evening, everybody. My name is Jane Franks and I'd like to welcome you all here this evening. It is my very great honour to introduce Joe Scott, mountain climber and adventurer, who is here to talk to us about his latest expedition – climbing Mount Kanchengjunga. Let's give him a warm welcome.

**Joe:** Thank you, thank you very much. It's a pleasure to be here. I love talking about my passion – mountain climbing – so I was absolutely delighted to receive the invitation to come and talk to you all this evening! So, as Jane mentioned, I've recently arrived back from climbing Mount Kanchengjunga.

Now, before I start, just out of interest, let's have a quick show of hands. Who here knows anything about Mount Kanchengjunga? Oh, OK, good to see that there are a few hands up at least! But, as I thought, this is a mountain that not many people are familiar with – even though it's one of the highest in the world and one of the most dangerous to climb. So I'd like to start by telling you a little more about it. It's 8586 metres high and it's on the border between Nepal and India. It's the third highest mountain in the world after Everest and K2, but in terms of difficulty of climbing, it's generally considered harder to climb than Everest, which is 262 metres higher, and it's just as difficult as K2, which is 25 metres higher.

My group and I went up the southwest face of the mountain at the head of the Yalung Valley. The route we took was along a snow ramp until we reached the West Ridge and then upward to the summit. The last push was really extreme and involved some very tough climbing. When we got to the top, we didn't walk on the summit itself out of respect for the local Sikkimese people who consider it to be sacred. The first team to climb the mountain (a British expedition led by Charles Evans in 1955) made a promise to the Maharaja of Sikkim that human feet would not walk on the summit when they climbed it, so we decided that we should honour this promise, too.

As I already mentioned, Kanchengjunga is one of the most dangerous mountains in the world to climb – the main risks are from avalanches and bad weather. We were very lucky that we didn't have either during our climb. Another problem is that there is no easy route to the top – whichever way you go, you have to cross some very difficult ground. And also, once you get to the top, you're not guaranteed to get back safely. Not every mountaineer has been as fortunate as we were – more than 20% of people who have tried to climb Kanchengjunga have lost their lives.

Now, people often ask me why I risk my life to reach new heights, so I thought I'd try and answer that for you here tonight. I wouldn't describe myself as reckless or a thrill-seeker. In contrast, I am focused and disciplined. I love what I do and I've spent years of my life training for it. What I feel when I reach the summit is not the adrenalin rush that other climbers talk about, but rather a real sense of achievement and the realisation of how powerful nature is. I feel truly peaceful – it's almost like meditation. Some people think that extreme sportspeople have to be risk takers. I disagree. I don't take risks – risk is all about uncertainty and not being in control. I do everything I can to reduce the risks and would never put myself in a situation where I'm not in control.

So to finish, I would say that my climb up Mount Kanchengjunga was one of the most rewarding experiences of my life. Now I'm going to go away and plan my next adventure! Maybe it'll be K2 next! Does anyone have any questions …?

## UNIT 11

### Track 26

1  Both photographs are alike in that they were taken in New York City.
2  In Photograph A, the subject is a person, while in Photograph B the subject is the city.
3  In Photograph A, it's daytime, whereas in Photograph B it's dusk.
4  Another point of difference is the area of the city that the photographs show. One is of a bridge over the river and the other is of a street and skyscrapers.
5  Photograph A is very bright and, in contrast, Photograph B is dark.
6  One similarity is that there are skyscrapers in both photographs.

## UNIT 12

### Track 27

1  Rio was great; however, we didn't get to visit Sugarloaf Mountain.
2  I love travelling for pleasure, but I really don't enjoy business travel.
3  Although it was very crowded, we enjoyed visiting the Louvre Museum in Paris.
4  London was a lot of fun despite the fact that it rained almost every day.
5  We decided to go to Shanghai despite not speaking any Chinese.
6  Things have cost a little more than we'd expected. Nevertheless, we've had a fantastic holiday.

### Track 28

**Danni:** Have you decided what you're doing this summer, Sarah?

**Sarah:** I'm going to China. My grandparents came from there, you know, so I'd really like to see it.

**Danni:** That's so cool, Sarah! Where are you going to go?

**Sarah:** I'm going to go to Beijing. I still have a lot of family there.

**Danni:** So do you speak any Chinese?

**Sarah:** Well, yeah, a little. My mother speaks Chinese really well and she spoke it to me when I was a kid.

**Danni:** I bet you'll have a great time.

**Sarah:** Oh, yeah. The history and the architecture there are amazing. There's the Great Wall, of course, which isn't far from the city, and there's the Forbidden City and the Summer Palace, but at the same time there are ultra-modern skyscrapers everywhere. I'm really, really into that kind of contrast. Have you ever been to Asia?

**Danni:** Yeah, sort of. When my family visited Australia, our plane stopped in Japan for a day, in Tokyo. I loved it! Of course it's probably very different from Beijing.

**Sarah:** True. But both are big, exciting, crowded cities.

**Danni:** Yeah. So where do your cousins live in Beijing?

**Sarah:** That's the best part. They're right in the centre.

**Danni:** What, you mean you're going to be living in the middle of the city?

**Sarah:** Yeah. My cousin's flat is right in the cultural heart of Beijing, and it's also near lots of amazing shopping and food on this street called *Wangfujing*.

**Danni:** That'll be great.

**Sarah:** Yeah, and one of my cousins has already said she wants to teach me all about Chinese cooking.

**Danni:** Oh, wow! You've got to come to my house and cook for me when you get back!

**Sarah:** I would love to cook you some Chinese food when I get back. Anyway, so what are you doing this summer?

**Danni:** I'm definitely going to find a job. I just don't know where I'm going to be working.

**Sarah:** What kind of job?

**Danni:** Anything, really.

**Sarah:** Hey, I know a guy who works at a little bookshop in the city centre. He might need someone.

**Danni:** Hey, I'd work in a bookshop. It'd probably be nice and quiet, and I could do a lot of reading!

**Sarah:** You'd probably get free coffee, too. They have a little café in there. It's called Greenhouse Books. It's in a little alley off the High Street. I'd be happy to introduce you.

### Track 29

Good morning, everyone. The topic for my presentation today is cities, specifically the *future* of cities. People have always loved to imagine what the cities of the future will be like. Back in the 1970s, for instance, after so many successful trips to space, scientists were fairly certain that by the year 2000, there would be a city on the moon and that this would be the first step in solving the overcrowding here on earth. And at that time, other experts who were concerned about air pollution, predicted that by the year 2008, some large cities would actually have domes over them. Obviously, those predictions weren't *completely* accurate.

Of course, it's very easy to laugh at these predictions, but the people who made them were very serious, and they were attempting to address very significant challenges like overcrowding and pollution. And, obviously, we still face those problems today. We love and celebrate the world's great cities, but at the same time we also know that they have their problems: they can be incredibly polluted or extremely overcrowded – and sometimes both, unfortunately.

So, even though earlier predictions have not come true, there is still an important question to consider. Will future cities solve problems like pollution and overcrowding? To address that question, I'd like to discuss some of the predictions that scientists today are making about the cities of 2050.

First, pollution. We know this is a problem in some cities, where it's sometimes dangerous just to go outside. However, some experts predict that the city of 2050 is going to have cleaner air. That's because we'll probably all be driving electric cars, which don't pollute the air like today's cars that use petrol. Some of you may be thinking that this is another unrealistic prediction that won't come true. After all, currently there are very few electric cars on the roads and they are too expensive for most drivers, but that's going to change in the coming decades. For one thing, petrol may be relatively affordable today, but it is going to become extremely expensive as the world's supply of oil is reduced. Then, at the same time, electric cars will become cheaper to manufacture. So we'll have more electric cars and the air will be cleaner, but there will still be terrible traffic. Great. Now that we've discussed pollution, let's turn to another problem facing cities of the future: overcrowding. All over the world, this problem is getting worse. Some experts think that by 2030, over 5 billion of the world's people will be living in cities.

So in 2050, what will cities be doing about overcrowding? To address the problem, some experts believe that we will actually be building new cities under the ocean. It sounds like science fiction, but there is already research on this idea. In the 1960s and 70s, the US Navy's Sealab program experimented with having divers live for weeks at a time under the water. Other countries carried out similar experiments at that time. Since it certainly isn't likely that cities will become less crowded, it's very possible that we may be forced to live in cities under the ocean by 2050. In that case, I suppose we won't be driving electric cars. Maybe electric submarines, though.

Now, what about even further in the future, 100 years from now? Many experts believe that as the world's cities continue to grow, the planet will have even more limited natural resources. If this happens, people will need to build cities in space or on other planets. One place to go might be the moon. Scientists recently discovered a cave on the moon that could be the perfect place to start a settlement. How many of you would like to live there? No one? Well, maybe *that* city won't be overcrowded!

# Answer key

## UNIT 1

### Section 1
**Exercise A**
1 Text 1: d   Text 2: a
2 Text 1: b   Text 2: a, c

**Exercise B**
1 F   2 F   3 T   4 T   5 F   6 T

### Section 2
**Exercise A**
1 social group   2 life goals
3 family values   4 sense
5 family background
6 social status

### Section 3
**Exercise A**
1 Lisa Adams   2 Lisa Adams
3 Mark Owens   4 Lisa Adams
5 Mark Owens   6 Mark Owens

**Exercise B**
6 I couldn't agree more.
1 Yes and no.
4 In a sense, you're right.
5 Well, yes, to a certain extent, but …
2 I'm sorry, but I just don't think that's true.
3 I'm afraid I can't agree.

### Section 4
**Exercise A**
✓ 1, 3

**What's right?**
I had to wear a uniform when I was at school.

**Exercise B**
1 was wearing   2 didn't have
3 did have   4 didn't look like
5 had never worn   6 put on
7 did feel

### Section 5
**Exercise A**
1 V   2 V   3 N   4 A   5 A   6 A
7 N

**Exercise B**
1 make sense of
2 sense of humour   3 sensible
4 common sense   5 sensitive
6 sense   7 sensitive

### Section 6
**Exercise A**
1 P   2 P   3 PP

**What's right?**
I was always taking pictures to express myself.

**Exercise B**
1 I used to try to be part of the 'cool' group
2 I would always do what my friends told me to do.
3 I was always behaving irresponsibly.
4 I never used to have a strong sense of my own identity.
5 I would never feel confident.

**Exercise C**
1 would work/used to work
2 would never help/never used to help
3 was always doing/always used to do/would always do
4 was always making sure/always used to make sure/would always make sure
5 would never take time off/never used to take time off

### SkillsStudio
**Exercise A**
1 there are many
2 more than one
3 three

**Exercise B**
1 F   2 C   3 A   4 E   5 D

**Exercise C**
1 d   2 c   3 a   4 b   5 b   6 a

**Exercise D**
Students' own answers

## UNIT 2

### Section 1
**Exercise A**
1 the economy
2 the service industry
3 trade
4 communications

**Exercise B**
Speaker 1 e, d, a
Speaker 2 c, a, d
Speaker 3 d, b, e

**Exercise C**
1 well   2 kind of   3 like
4 I mean   5 you know

### Section 2
**Exercise A**
1 d   2 b   3 f   4 a   5 e   6 c

**Exercise B**
1 multinational
2 economic growth   3 dominate
4 profits   5 regional   6 facilitates

### Section 3
**Exercise A**
1 have   2 are you seeing
3 think   4 are

**Exercise B**
My girlfriend and I had (1) ~~seen~~ **been seeing** each other for three years when her company offered her a job in the Shanghai office. It was (2) ~~being~~ an amazing opportunity, so she moved there last September, and we (3) ~~are not seeing~~ **haven't seen** each other very often since then. It isn't (4) ~~being~~ ideal, but there are a lot of ways to keep in touch. And we've just got engaged, so I (5) ~~'m thinking~~ **think** that old saying, 'absence makes the heart grow fonder', might just be true!

**What's right?**
I am/I'm thinking of applying for a transfer to the Stockholm office next year.

### Section 4
**Exercise A**
1 c   2 e   3 a   4 b   5 f   6 d

**Exercise B**
a 2e, 3a, 5f
b 1c, 4b, 6d

**Exercise C**
1 a   2 b   3 b   4 a   5 a   6 b
7 b

**What's right?**
Multinational companies are becoming more and more dominant.

### Section 5
**Exercise A**
1 support   2 promote
3 campaign   4 generate   5 value
6 sustain   7 participate   8 boost

**Exercise B**
1 a   2 b   3 b   4 c   5 c   6 a
7 b   8 c

## Section 6

**Exercise A**

1 Dear Mr Moreno,
2 Thank you for your interest in
3 Could you let me know
4 You will be required to attend
5 I look forward to meeting you
6 Regards
7 Klaus Steinmann, Director, globe4u

**Exercise B**

(1) ~~Hi Klaus!~~ **Dear Mr Steinmann,**
(2) ~~Thanks so much~~ **Thank you** for your email.
I would prefer to work in June rather than August and I'm available to come in to discuss the work on 5th May at 10 am. (3) ~~Just tell me~~ **Could you let me know** if there's any preparation that I can do for the meeting?
(4) ~~See you then.~~ **I look forward to meeting you**.
(5) ~~With love~~, **Regards,**
(6) ~~Miguel~~ **Miguel Moreno**

## SkillsStudio

**Exercise A**

c

**Exercise B**

2 The harm that tourism can do to the environment.
1 What an ethical tourist is.
4 How to be an ethical tourist.
3 The harm that tourism can do to local communities.

**Exercise C**

**How can tourism harm the environment?**

1 There are more carbon emissions from increased air travel.
2 Tourists damage local environment by dropping rubbish.
3 Tourism uses too many natural resources, such as water.

**How can tourism harm local communities?**

1 Local businesses can't compete with multinational companies.
2 People are forced out of their homes to make way for tourism.

**How can we become ethical tourists?**

1 Use ethical transportation (trains, boats, bicycles) if possible.

2 Leave excess packaging at home.
3 Make sure your travel operator is ethical.

**Exercise D**

1 b  2 c  3 a  4 f  5 d  6 e

**Exercise E**

1 a  2 b  3 a  4 c  5 b

**Exercise F**

Students' own answers

# UNIT 3

## Section 1

**What's right?**

She told us she had to work late yesterday.

**Exercise A**

2 had never tried
3 couldn't believe/might meet
4 had to take
5 shouldn't charge
6 would probably never be

**Exercise B**

1 would/will  2 might  3 couldn't
4 had planned  5 would  6 could
7 has to/had to  8 could  9 should

## Section 2

**Exercise A**

1 fortune  2 record  3 scandal
4 invention  5 company  6 a cure
7 novel

**Exercise B**

a 6  b 4  c 2  d 7  e 5  f 3  g 1

## Section 3

**Exercise A**

1 b  2 c  3 a

**Exercise B**

1 b; Times Education Supplement
2 b; childhood obesity
3 a; He thinks that one part of the government is investing in food education and healthy school lunches while the other part is promoting junk food and allowing it to be sold near schools.
4 b; TV chef Jamie Oliver
5 c; 16th May
6 a; He believes that it's important to teach children how to cook because it's an essential life skill that can help their future health and wellbeing.

## Section 4

1 a  2 a  3 a  4 b  5 b  6 a
7 b  8 a

## Section 5

**What's right?**

They said she would never be famous but years later she became a big star.

**Exercise A**

1 O  2 O  3 O  4 N  5 O

**Exercise B**

a 1, 5  b 3  c 2  d 4

**Exercise C**

She said that Jay Z was never going to be a successful rapper.

**Exercise D**

1 she's probably not going to win/ she probably wasn't going to win
2 wants/wanted
3 she's wearing/she was wearing
4 dreams/dreamed
5 isn't/wasn't
6 would never be
7 will cry/would cry

## Section 6

**Exercise A**

1 Actually, that's not what I meant.
2 Fame isn't easy, put it that way.
3 Maybe I'm not making myself clear.
4 Perhaps I should rephrase that.
5 What I meant was, it's complicated.
6 What I'm trying to say is, it's a problem.

**Exercise B**

1 e  2 a  3 d  4 b  5 c  6 f

## SkillsStudio

**Exercise A**

1 Winston Churchill
2 Sherlock Holmes, King Arthur, Winston Churchill

**Exercise B**

1 confusion  2 fictional
3 treasure  4 inspired

**Exercise C**

1 e  2 d  3 a  4 b

**Exercise D**

1 f  2 h  3 a  4 g  5 e  6 b

**Exercise E**

Students' own answers

# UNIT 4

## Section 1
**Exercise A**
1 F  2 F  3 F  4 T  5 F  6 T

**Exercise B**
a 3  b 2  c 1  d 7  e 10  f 9
g 6  h 8  i 5  j 11  k 12  l 4

**Exercise C**
1 c, e, i,  2 d, f, k  3 b, h, j
4 a, g, l

## Section 2
**Exercise A**
**Nouns:** appreciation,
contentment, enjoyment,
happiness, pleasure, satisfaction,
wealth
**Adjectives:** content, happy,
pleasant, wealthy
**Verbs:** appreciate, enjoy, satisfy

**Exercise B**
1 enjoy  2 wealthy
3 satisfaction/pleasure
4 content/happy  5 appreciate
6 happiness/pleasure/
contentment  7 pleasant

## Section 3
**Exercise A**
1 when  2 why  3 how
4 where  5 what

**Exercise B**
1 b  2 c  3 a  4 c  5 b

**Exercise C**
1 what  2 why  3 when  4 where
5 how

**What's right?**
I don't know where he went.

## Section 4
**Exercise A**
1 pessimistic  2 depressed
3 state of well-being
4 optimistic  5 in a good mood
6 distracted  7 emotions
8 focused

**Exercise B**
1 distracted, focused
2 optimistic, pessimistic
3 emotions, state of well-being
4 depressed, in a good mood

## Section 5
**Exercise A**
1 present simple
2 present simple
3 past simple
4 past perfect

**Exercise B**
1 would have cried, had watched
2 sees, will/'ll tell
3 were, would/'d be
4 had told, could have helped
5 have, help
6 don't take, will/'ll regret

**What's right?**
If you had/'d told me he was
depressed, I would have called
him.

**Exercise C**
Sian:  What are you reading?
Lisa:  It's an article called *The Key
       to Happiness*. I **(1) will/'ll**
       read you some sections if
       you're interested.
Sian:  All right.
Lisa:  OK, well, it says that if
       you **(2)** ~~wanted~~ **want** to
       be happy, then be a good
       friend because, strong
       relationships are the key to
       contentment.
Sian:  I think that's true. I love
       spending time with my
       friends and if I didn't have
       them, I **(3)** ~~will~~ **would** be very
       unhappy.
Lisa:  Me, too. It also says that
       people are usually more
       satisfied with life if they
       **(4)** ~~did~~ **do** a job that they
       love.
Sian:  Yeah, that's true, too. Do
       you remember last year
       when I was doing that office
       job I hated? If I hadn't got a
       new job in the music store,
       I **(5)** ~~will~~ **would/'d** still be
       miserable.
Lisa:  Hmm, and probably the
       reason I'm not that happy
       right now is because I don't
       have a job I enjoy. I think
       if I **(6)** ~~have~~ **had** a job that I
       loved, then I would be more
       content.

Sian:  I totally agree. So,
       stop reading that article and
       check out the job listings
       instead!
Lisa:  Good point!

## Section 6
**Exercise A**
1 Your donation was so generous.
2 I would also like to express my
gratitude for …
3 Thanks again from all of us here.
4 I am writing to thank you for …

**Exercise B**
1 I am writing to thank you for
2 Your donation was so generous
3 I would also like to express my
gratitude for
4 Thanks again from all of us here.

## SkillsStudio
**Exercise A**
1 pessimistic
2 optimistic
3 optimistic

**Exercise B**
1 23, 69  2 Speaker 3

**Exercise C**
1 b  2 e  3 d  4 a  5 c  6 f

**Exercise D**
1 high  2 agrees  3 declining
4 doesn't say  5 low  6 disagrees
7 increasing  8 doesn't say
9 high  10 agrees  11 declining
12 agrees

**Exercise E**
1 a  2 a  3 b  4 b  5 c  6 d

**Exercise F**
Students' own answers

# UNIT 5

## Section 1
**Exercise A**
1 e  2 d  3 a  4 c  5 b

**What's right?**
Dozens of homes were damaged
by the flood.

## Exercise B
1 was first built
2 was awarded
3 has been transformed
4 are being added
5 is now called
6 was designed
7 hadn't been abandoned
8 was redesigned
9 has been visited
10 is still being used

## Exercise C
1 is located
2 was built
3 was given
4 are painted
5 has recently been decorated / was recently decorated
6 has recently been planted / was recently planted
7 are always served
8 had been cleared away

## Section 2
### Exercise A
1 c   2 a   3 b
### Exercise B
1 a   2 b   3 a   4 b   5 a   6 a

## Section 3
### Exercise A
c
### Exercise B
1 range from … to …
5 market … as …
2 to make … worth …
3 put up against …
4 as much about … as …
### Exercise C
1 **ranges from** €2.00 **to** €3.50
2 **market** bottled water **as** something
3 **as much about** helping the planet **as** our own convenience
4 **put** bottled water **up against** other products
5 **To make** a simple bottle of water **worth** that kind of money

## Section 4
### Exercise A
1 collecting   2 putting
3 displaying   4 is   5 giving
6 take   7 hand

## Section 5
### Exercise A
1 *for* + gerund
2 *in order (not) to* + base form
3 *so as (not) to* + base form
4 *so (that)* + (pro)noun + clause
5 *to* + base form
### Exercise B
1 for
2 to / in order to / so as to
3 for
4 To / In order to / So as to
5 so / so that
6 So as not to / In order not to
### What's right?
Everyone must drink water to stay healthy.

## Section 6
### Exercise A
1 water pollution   2 famine
3 hygiene   4 flood
5 water poverty   6 drought
7 disease   8 climate change
### Exercise B
1 water poverty
2 water pollution   3 hygiene
4 diseases   5 climate change
6 floods   7 droughts   8 famine

## SkillsStudio
### Exercise A
2 Water footprinting – a new approach to water conservation
### Exercise B
2 The total volume of fresh water used to produce goods and services
### Exercise C
1 …most of us know the concept of the carbon footprint.
2 There is, however, another global environmental issue that requires urgent international attention: water resources.
3 As a way of drawing society's attention to the nature and scale of the problem, scientists have developed the concept of the 'water footprint'.
4 Water footprints can be calculated for specific goods and products.
5 Water footprints have also been calculated for each nation, with the result that we can compare international water consumption.

## Exercise D
1 c   2 b   3 a   4 c   5 a
### Exercise E
Students' own answers

# UNIT 6

## Section 1
### Exercise A
1 'm used to   2 get used to
3 got used to   4 get used to
5 wasn't used to   6 got used to
### Exercise B
1 am/'m getting used to
2 to get used to
3 am/'m used to
4 am/'m used to
5 to get used to
6 am/'m used to
### What's right?
I'm used to travelling for my job.

## Section 2
### Exercise A
1 b   2 a   3 b
### Exercise B
Speaker 1 b   Speaker 2 d
Speaker 3 c   Speaker 4 a

## Section 3
### Exercise A
1 fresher   2 initiation   3 mascot
4 high-ranking   5 ritual
6 symbolic
### Exercise B
1 ritual   2 initiation   3 symbolic
4 fresher   5 mascot
6 high-ranking
### Exercise C
1 freshers   2 initiation   3 ritual
4 mascot   5 high-ranking
6 symbolic

## Section 4
### Exercise A
1 Did he invite you to go to his graduation party?
2 I advise you not to be late for morning exercises.
3 The principal ordered the students to be quiet.
4 They expect the freshers to arrive on time for the ceremony.

## Exercise B

1 us not to worry   2 us to review
3 us to get   4 us to use
5 us not to bring
6 us to come / us to go

**What's right?**
They even ask us not to work too hard.

## Section 5
### Exercise A

1 e   2 d   3 f   4 c   5 g   6 b
7 h   8 a

### Exercise B

1 go through   2 plan out
3 put on   4 writing down
5 go over   6 cross off
7 line up   8 clean out

## Section 6
### Exercise A

The following sentences should be underlined.
I just returned from a walk in the woods, every New Year's Day I put on my walking boots and walk in the same place.
I like it, it means I go back there every year on the anniversary of his death and remember him.
I have a personal ritual for when I am worried, I buy a balloon.
This reminds them that I'm thinking about them, it reminds them that they aren't going through life alone.
Now, every morning, I remember my promise, I put on my ring.
I don't have any rituals, now I'll try to start one.

### Exercise B

Suggested answers. (Note that the semi-colon, the full stop and the word *and* could be used in any of the sentences, but the following answers show the ways to use all the options.)
1 I just returned from a walk in the woods. Every New Year's Day I put on my hiking boots and walk in the same place.
2 I like it, because it means I go back there every year on the anniversary of his death and remember him.

3 I have a personal ritual for when I am worried; I buy a balloon.
4 This reminds them that I'm thinking about them, and it reminds them that they aren't going through life alone.
5 Now, every morning, I remember my promise when I put on my ring.
6 I don't have any rituals, but now I'll try to start one.

### SkillsStudio
**Exercise A**

1 Monkey Buffet Festival (C)
2 Cheese-Rolling Festival (A)
3 La Tomatina (E)
4 Up Helly Aa (B)
5 Konaki Sumo Festival (D)

**Exercise B**

1 d   2 h   3 f   4 c   5 a   6 e
7 b   8 g

**Exercise C**

1 c   2 h   3 b   4 f   5 e

**Exercise D**

1 Monkey Buffet Festival, Thailand, A large picnic is held for the many monkeys that live locally.
2 Cheese-Rolling Festival, England, Competitors race to see who can catch a large round cheese as it rolls down a hill.
3 La Tomatina, Spain, A large food fight happens where people throw overripe tomatoes at each other.
4 Up Helly Aa, the island of Shetland, Scotland, There is a parade with torches and a boat is then burned. Then there is entertainment in venues across the town.
5 Konaki Sumo, Japan, Two Sumo wrestlers hold two babies. The first baby to cry is the winner.

**Exercise E**
Students' own answers

# UNIT 7

## Section 1
### Exercise A

1 top-quality   2 template
3 manufacture   4 miniature
5 unique   6 innovative
7 affordable   8 personalised

### Exercise B

1 unique   2 innovative
3 template   4 miniature
5 manufacture   6 affordable
7 top quality   8 personalised

## Section 2
### Exercise A

1 c   2 f   3 a   4 b   5 d   6 e

**What's right?**
He designs affordable, comfortable children's clothes.

### Exercise B

1 Dolce and Gabbana's
2 girls', boys'
3 company's closing
4 designers' mothers'
5 designer's and CEO's

### Exercise C

1 star's   2 celebrities'   3 ✗
4 sister's   5 husband's   6 site's
7 ✗   8 ✗   9 ✗   10 Adidas'
11 Gucci's

## Section 3
### Exercise A

✓ 1, 4, 5, 6, 8

### Exercise B

1 If you're like most people, the thought of painting the walls doesn't exactly fill your heart with happiness and joy. (paragraph 1)
4 … babies cry more in yellow rooms. (paragraph 2)
5 … blue interiors can lower blood pressure and reduce your heart rate. For this reason, many people choose this relaxing colour for their bedrooms. (paragraph 3)
6 … create an exciting atmosphere and get people talking … especially at night … (paragraph 4)
8 … brings together the best qualities of blue and yellow. (paragraph 5)

## Section 4
### Exercise A

1 out   2 off   3 with   4 up
5 on   6 to

### Exercise B

1 brought out   2 coming up with
3 drew up   4 caught on
5 took off   6 look up to

## Section 5

**Exercise A**

1 had ended
2 had been drawing up
3 had opened
4 had been
5 had been waiting/had waited
6 had been coming up with

**What's right?**

She didn't show anyone her designs until she had finished them.

**Exercise B**

1 had made/had been making
2 had changed
3 had attended/had been attending
4 had noticed
5 had asked
6 had thought

## Section 6

**Exercises A and B**

1 I was hoping
2 I was thinking we
3 I wanted to suggest
4 I was wondering

**Exercise C**

1 I wanted to ask your opinion about painting the bathroom blue.
2 I think we should buy a new rug to match the colour of the sofa.
3 I was hoping my mother would help us by coming up with an idea of how to decorate the baby's room.
4 I was wondering if Maria had any suggestions for an interesting design for the kitchen.

## SkillsStudio

**Exercise A**

a to amuse readers with stories about the building's problems

**Exercise B**

1 gawk   2 dispute   3 ray
4 context   5 overcast   6 spire
7 awning   8 glare   9 suspend
10 scorch

**Exercise C**

a 2   b 4   c 5   d 1   e 6   f 3

**Exercise D**

Students' own answers

# UNIT 8

## Section 1

**Exercise A**

1 poverty   2 ambassador
3 philanthropic   4 humanitarian
5 refugee   6 injustice
7 underprivileged   8 foundation

**Exercise B**

1 refugee   2 poverty   3 injustice
4 ambassador   5 underprivileged
6 philanthropic   7 foundation
8 humanitarian

## Section 2

**Exercise A**

1 Sam would prefer not to take part in the demonstration tomorrow.
2 ✓
3 They would prefer donations not to be sent by mail.
4 ✓
5 We would rather she didn't volunteer anywhere dangerous.
6 We'd prefer not to collect donations until tomorrow.

**What's right?**

I'd rather donate time than money.

**Exercise B**

1 not to receive   2 gave   3 went
4 not to transport   5 invest
6 to see

## Section 3

**Exercise A and B**

a 3   b 2   c 1

**Exercise C**

Main idea 1 b
Main idea 2 a
Main idea 3 c

**Exercise D**

1 doesn't make   2 sell   3 70
4 the USA   5 Overseas Needlepoint and Crafts Project
6 North America   7 50   8 2006

## Section 4

**Exercise A**

1 d   2 f   3 a   4 b   5 e   6 c

**Exercise B**

1 has the right to
2 can't afford to
3 unemployed
4 benefits
5 have a responsibility to
6 live on

## Section 5

**Exercise A**

1 b   2 a   3 a   4 b   5 b   6 a

**What's right?**

What the charity needs is …

**Exercise B**

1 What people need is a way to feed themselves.
2 Who receives the most aid is uncertain.
3 Where we send donations this year is undecided.
4 What we do is distribute baskets of food.
5 How we support our community is important.
6 What's best is to donate money direct.

## Section 6

**Exercise A**

1 c   2 a   3 g   4 e   5 d
6 b   7 f

**Exercise B**

1 Discovering how many homeless people there are in your area may surprise you.
2 What they really need is your support to help them get back on their feet.
3 But it's not always easy to know how to get involved in charity work.
4 If you volunteer in some way, you could make a significant contribution.
5 Charities, which often need volunteers, may be the main source of funding for local homeless shelters.
6 You could think of new and exciting ways of getting people to donate money to the charity.

## SkillsStudio

**Exercise A**

a Because he wanted to show the US government how it can help deal with violence in the Democratic Republic of Congo.

**Exercise B**

1 Rosie   2 Paul

**Exercise C**

1 b   2 c   3 a   4 b   5 a   6 b
7 c   8 b

**Exercise D**
1 f   2 a   3 g   4 b   5 d   6 c
7 e   8 h

**Exercise E**
1 join   2 hear   3 respond
4 disagree   5 point   6 agree

**Exercise F**
a 1, 3   b 2, 5   c 4, 6

**Exercise G**
Students' own answers

# UNIT 9

## Section 1
**Exercise A**
1 about, to   2 at, about   3 by
4 about, in   5 about, about

**What's right?**
As a parent, I object to having beauty contests for children. Would you like to play football in the park on Sunday?

**Exercise B**
1 looking   2 interested
3 capable   4 object   5 insist
6 happy   7 bored   8 excited
9 responsible

## Section 2
**Exercise A**
b, d

**Exercise B**
a 2   b 3   c 1   d 4

**Exercise C**
a 2   b 3, 4   c 1

## Section 3
1 a feeling of   2 a desire to
3 the agony of   4 the fun of
5 the will to

## Section 4
**Exercise A**
Every evening, millions of families around the world sit at home **watching** reality TV. We know we shouldn't waste time **watching** these programmes, but we have a good time **laughing** at them. They're harmless fun. Or are they? According to a recent survey of girls aged 11–17, those who like to watch reality TV are more competitive than the girls who don't. They are more likely to agree with statements such as,

'You have to lie to get what you want', 'I have a hard time **trusting** other girls' and 'It's normal for girls to gossip and compete with each other'. However, the effects of reality TV were not all negative. Sixty-two percent of the girls who watched reality said they found themselves **learning** about new things and important issues.

**What's right?**
Olympic athletes spent years preparing for this opportunity.

**Exercise B**
1 have trouble   2 performing
3 listening   4 spend   5 sit
6 find   7 solving   8 thinking

## Section 5
1 Research   2 prove   3 studies
4 researching   5 conclusions
6 theory   7 experiments
8 measure   9 tested

## Section 6
**Exercise A**
1 a   2 b   3 a   4 a

## SkillsStudio
**Exercise A**
1 should not   2 should not
3 should

**Exercise B**
1 c   2 a   3 b, d   4 b   5 a

**Exercise C**
1 F   2 T   3 NM   4 NM
5 F   6 T

**Exercise D**
Students' own answers

# UNIT 10

## Section 1
**Exercise A**
1 be exposed to   2 dare to
3 failure   4 freedom
5 play it safe   6 risky   7 security
8 take a chance

**Exercise B**
1 freedom, security
2 risky, took a chance
3 are/'re exposed to, play it safe
4 dared to, failure

## Section 2
**Exercise A**
1 G   2 G   3 I   4 B   5 G   6 B
7 I   8 I   9 G

**Exercise B**
1 a   2 c   3 c   4 a   5 c
6 a   7 b

**What's right?**
You have to be capable of taking risks to run your own business.

## Section 3
**Exercise A**
1 a   2 b   3 c

**Exercise B**
a We would like you to consider …
b We are writing to draw your attention to a problem we noticed …
c We are confident that you will take prompt action regarding this matter.
d We would like to mention that we are happy with …

**Exercise C**
Dear Mrs Carter,
3 (1 d) We would like to mention that we are happy with the decision to install a lift in the shopping centre because it is very useful for elderly people like myself and saves us having to climb the stairs! (2 c) We are confident that you will take prompt action regarding this matter.
2 (3 a) We would like you to consider taking the following action:
– Close off the lift so that children can't play in it.
– Fix the lift as soon as possible.
1 (4 b) We are writing to draw your attention to a problem we noticed in the new shopping centre – the lift is broken and children were playing in it, which is dangerous.

## Section 4
**Exercise A**
1 f   2 d   3 b   4 a   5 c   6 e

**Exercise B**
1 risk their lives   2 risky
3 risk assessment
4 reduce the risks
5 run the risk   6 at risk

### Section 5

**Exercise A**

1 SI  2 MP  3 SP  4 MP  5 SI
6 SI  7 MP

**Exercise B**

1 must have  2 couldn't have
3 may have  4 could have
5 might have  6 must have

**Exercise C**

1 can't have been
2 might have fallen off
3 might have thrown
4 could have had
5 may not have seemed
6 could have been

**What's right?**

He couldn't have thought it was risky, or he wouldn't have done it.

### Section 6

**Exercise A**

2

**Exercise B**

1 T  2 F  3 T  3 T

**Exercise C**

1 Did  2 must have  3 got to
4 kind of  5 want to
6 don't know  7 could have
8 got a

### SkillsStudio

**Exercise A**

1 third  2 Nepal  3 1955

**Exercise B**

b his most recent expedition and his motivation for climbing mountains

**Exercise C**

2 Joe's climb up Mount Kanchengjunga
1 Facts and figures about Mount Kanchengjunga
5 Joe's plans for the future
3 The dangers associated with Mount Kanchengjunga
4 The reasons why Joe loves climbing

**Exercise D**

1 c  2 f  3 a  4 e  5 b  6 d

**Exercise E**

1 put up/raise their hands
2 8586 m, third
3 higher/taller, easier
4 southwest
5 avalanches and bad weather
6 More than 20%
7 doesn't think/doesn't agree/disagrees
8 rewarding

**Exercise F**

Students' own answers

## UNIT 11

### Section 1

**Exercise A**

1 F  2 A  3 D  4 C  5 B

**Exercise B**

1 C  2 A  3 F  4 D  5 B

### Section 2

1 landscape  2 subject
3 left-hand side  4 foreground
5 right-hand side  6 portrait
7 background  8 out of focus
9 in focus

### Section 3

1 similar in that  2 similarities
3 whereas  4 unlike  5 similar
6 while

### Section 4

**Exercise A**

1 b  2 a

**Exercise B**

1 A  2 A  3 C  4 A  5 C
6 A  7 C  8 C  9 A  10 C
11 C  12 C  13 A

**Exercise C**

1 because  2 As a consequence,
3 So,  4 because  5 because of
6 In addition to  7 Therefore,

**What's right?**

Lots of people want to be thinner because of selfies.

### Section 5

**Exercise A**

1 b  2 f  3 e  4 c  5 h  6 g
7 d  8 a

**Exercise B**

1 To explain a similarity between two things: 2f, 6g, 8a
2 To explain a difference between two things: 1b, 3e, 4c, 5h, 7d

**Exercise C**

1 S  2 D  3 D  4 D  5 D  6 S
7 D  8 S

### Section 6

**Exercise A**

1 c  2 g  3 f  4 b  5 j  6 e
7 d  8 i  9 h  10 a

**Exercise B**

1 to inform  2 driving  3 meeting
4 to reply  5 to fix  6 to buy
7 eating  8 swimming  9 seeing
10 to get

**What's right?**

I forgot to hand in my assignment this morning.

### SkillsStudio

**Exercise A**

1 negative  2 negative
3 positive

**Exercise B**

1 a  2 b  3 a  4 b  5 a  6 a
7 a  8 b

**Exercise C**

1 B  2 B, D  3 A  4 C  5 A, D
6 B, D  7 B, C  8 A

**Exercise D**

Students' own answers

## UNIT 12

### Section 1

**Exercise A**

1 however  2 but  3 Although
4 despite the fact  5 despite
6 Nevertheless

**Exercise B**

Correct: 4, 5
Incorrect:
1 Rio was great; however, we didn't get to visit Sugarloaf Mountain./Rio was great. However, we didn't get to visit Sugarloaf Mountain.
2 I love travelling for pleasure, but I really don't enjoy business travel.
3 Although it was very crowded, we enjoyed visiting the Louvre Museum in Paris.
6 Things have cost a little more than we'd expected. Nevertheless, we've had a fantastic vacation./Things have cost a little more than we'd expected; nevertheless, we've had a fantastic vacation.

**What's right?**

Despite arriving / the fact that we arrived an hour late, my flight to Chicago went well.

**Exercise C**

1 Despite/In spite of
2 However/Nevertheless
3 Although/Even though
4 Although/Even though
5 However/Nevertheless
6 Despite/In spite of
7 although/even though
8 However/Nevertheless

## Section 2

1 disappointed, c
2 Dear, a
3 Furthermore, d
4 hearing, e
5 concerning, b
6 Yours faithfully, f

## Section 3

**Exercise A**

A 4   B 3   C 1   D 5   E 2

**Exercise B**

Paragraph A: b
Paragraph B: a
Paragraph E: c

**Exercise C**

1 Dear Sir/Madam
2 I am writing concerning
3 we were very disappointed with it
4 First of all
5 Furthermore
6 Finally
7 For these reasons
8 I enclose
9 I look forward to hearing from you
10 Yours faithfully

## Section 4

**Exercise A**

1 trade   2 heart   3 views
4 alley   5 heritage   6 village
7 site   8 settlement

**Exercise B**

1 heart   2 settlement   3 trade
4 heritage   5 village   6 site
7 views   8 alleys

## Section 5

**Exercise A**

1 plans for the future   2 travel
3 members of her family   4 shop

**Exercise B**

1 China
2 history and architecture
3 the centre
4 Chinese cooking
5 He wants to find a job.
6 working at a local bookshop

## Section 6

**Exercise A**

1 d   2 b   3 c   4 a

**What's right?**

By the time this concert ends, the trains and buses won't be running.

**Exercise B**

1 may be   2 are leaving
3 will prevent   4 may sink
5 may become
6 will be experiencing
7 are going to build   8 will be

## SkillsStudio

**Exercise A**

1 D   2 A   3 B   4 C

**Exercise B**

4 limited resources
3 overcrowding
2 climate change
1 pollution

**Exercise C**

limited resources, overcrowding, pollution

**Exercise D**

1 d   2 a   3 c   4 b   5 d

**Exercise E**

1, 2

**Exercise F**

Students' own answers